AMERICAN CULT NXIVM EXPOSED

OMAR W. ROSALES

Published in the United States of America
Library of Congress Cataloging Data Pending

Cover Design by Author
Publisher:
MyMinox Press LLC
PO Box 6429
Austin, TX
78762-6429

ISBN-13: 978-19-80985-74-7

Dedicated to the Women and Men of Law Enforcement.
And to destroying a Myth...

CONTENTS

Introduction   i

 1 American Roots   1
 2 Beginnings   25
 3 The Monster   34
 4 Invitation   42
 5 Arrival   45
 6 Mouth   47
 7 Walk   57
 8 Veil   67
 9 Belly   70
10 Reveal   78
11 Rise   88
12 Fallen   92
13 Sunlight   100

DOSSIER   107

BONUS MATERIALS   133

FBI Affidavit to Arrest   134
Keith Raniere

Letter Requesting Denial of   157
Bond For Keith Raniere

Psychological Profile of   170
a Modern Cult Leader

Letter from former Member   171
Of NXIVM and Scientology

ALTERNATIVE THEORY   173

INTRODUCTION

Somewhere in Texas
March 30, 2018

Business Insider Headline – Former 'Smallville' star reportedly linked to alleged cult

Daily Beast Headline – How 'Smallville' Actress Allison Mack became a Women-Branding Cult Leader

Daily Mail Headline– Former Smallville Actress Kristin Kreuk Has Broken Her Silence on Sex Cult

As I sit at my computer and write these words, never in a million years did I believe I would be telling my story. Keith Raniere, the leader of the NXIVM (pronounced Nexium) Cult was just arrested in Mexico under suspicion of sex slavery. The FBI Special Agent's probable cause affidavit, used as a basis for Keith's arrest and indictment, reveals a shocking story of sex, slavery, abuse, and degradation. (Author's Note: FBI documents are included in the Bonus Materials of this book).

Keith was flown from Puerto Vallarta, Mexico, where he had been staying at a $10,000-a-week private villa, to Federal Court in Fort Worth, Texas courtesy of the FBI. Through his attorneys, Raniere agrees to be transferred to Brooklyn, New York to await his indictment and trial in the Eastern District of New York.

He is charged with multiple violations of Federal law including sex slavery, human trafficking, and forced servitude. His bond will probably be denied and he may spend the rest of life in a SuperMax Federal prison.

I feel torn, because I know these people. I can call Keith 'Keith' and not his title 'Vanguard', because I know him. Allison Mack is 'Allie'. And some members of the group were (and still are) my friends. But, I want to tell my story and reveal the truth.

The truth about how I survived my encounter with a modern American cult...

1 AMERICAN ROOTS

The hallmark of the charismatic leader, is the ability to convince his followers to do something they would never do in real life. The majority of charismatic leaders are male, they appeal to followers that feel lost or unheard, and they preach messages of hope. Yet, beneath the facade of hope lies darkness. It is this darkness of control and lack of self-control that characterizes a modern cult.

Followers Led Astray – Donner Party

In the modern America era, the first instance where a charismatic leader damaged his followers occurred in 1846 with the Donner party. A great push of westward expansion occupied American thoughts. 'Go West young Man,' was a popular saying. Many felt that the American push was destiny made *manifest*. California offered hope and a prosperous future, as people migrated to the West via the Oregon trail. The Donner party started off as the last group, in the last wagon train headed west in the spring of 1846. Yet, the timing leaving Independence, Missouri was important. Leave too early, and the wagons will encounter the wet spring muds. Leave too late, and the party will face troubles with the early Fall snows.

At about the same time, a fellow named Lansford W. Hastings emerged. Hastings was a self-promoter, a reckless adventurer, and an opportunist. Contemporaries described him as a Baron Munchausen – a ridiculous braggart with no real-world experience. Hastings claimed there was a shortcut to the Oregon trail that would bypass Fort Hall and the Snake River in the Dakota territory, that would allow wagons to shave months off the trip to California. There were two obvious problems: 1) Hastings never before attempted the route himself and 2) the Hastings route meant crossing the Great Salt Lake desert in summer, when the evaporating water under the salt turned the trail gummy.

Through his powers of persuasion, Hastings talked up the ease and speed of his shortcut. Hastings even said there was resupply along the route (but he failed to mention that he was part owner of the trading post and would make a hefty profit from any wagon trains traveling through). To promote his new route, Hastings talked up the trail, posted flyers, and sent letters about his brilliant plan. Soon, he had a bite as the Donner party arrived in Fort Bridger. Yet, Hastings was no longer at the fort, he had already started his journey. The only thing that awaited the Donner party was another letter from Hastings.

The leader of the Donner party was George Donner. Donner was described as peaceful, charitable, and kind. Despite the pioneer image, most in the party were not suited for life in the rugged wilderness. Only a few had trades, the rest were middle-class folk. The party encountered difficulties from the start of the Hastings shortcut.

As the journey continued, the situation became worse. There was no resupply and many wagons were abandoned while crossing the gummy Salt Lake. First animals, then people starved. Sick or ill people were left behind on the trail. And none were suited for the harsh realities of crossing the Sierra Nevada in a such a perilous way. Finally back on the Oregon trail in September 1846, the Donner party could not beat the Fall snows and were trapped in the Sierra Nevada at a campsite later called Donner's Pass. Although the settlers found cabins, the flat roofs (and lack of building materials for insulation and warmth) proved disastrous.

Many of the Donner party died in the Winter of 1846. Lacking food, the members first ate animal hides, then roofing materials, then each other. The most shocking story, was that some members actually preferred the taste of human flesh, to the sickly animal carcasses that were frozen outside the cabins. When rescued, one member was found cooking a stew of human remains, while plenty of animal meat was outside.

Cults appeal to those who are lost or are having difficulties in life. Despair, lack of familial support, loss of job, and divorce are all times when people are vulnerable. These new 'prospective' members are looking for signposts along the journey. Shortcuts to happiness, if you will. Yet these perceived shortcuts only lead to more long-term misery.

Spiritualist Movement

The Spiritualist Movement began in the 1850s, as a confluence of Pentecostal religions (that acknowledged speaking in tongues and trance-like states) and the need to communicate with deceased loved ones. With perilous Westward migration, and more loss of life via the American Civil War, the national psyche was disconnected.

Americans needed comfort. Mediumship and Spiritualism offered a way to connect with long-lost souls of departed family members. Spiritualist teachings emphasized the immortal nature of the human soul. Spiritualist leaders used séances, mediumship, and materialization of spirit matter to prove that the souls of the dead, could cross over and speak to the living.

During a séance (always held in a dimly-lit room) the medium would enter a trance. In this trance state, the medium would then relay messages from the dead. Participants would also report hearing bells, music from nowhere, and materialization of artifacts or ectoplasm. Yet, the Spiritualist movement began to lose steam, as many mediums were exposed as frauds. The parlor tricks included cymbals tied to thighs, objects hidden under the table (later claimed as materialized spirit objects), and tables that could be easily lifted via a medium's legs. Spiritualism again gained prominence after World War I, as families yearned to connect with the souls of dead family members.

A cult will typically operate in the shadows and shun publicity. For the cult to function, it must separate its followers from society in order for the cult leader to spread the message. This separation is the modern version of the dimly-lit room. Pulled away from society, absent of critical thinking and questioning, this atmosphere allows a cult to flourish and control its members.

Flower Power and the 60s

The 1960s saw a decade of change as the Youth of America openly questioned the decision-making and authority of governments and leaders. Protests about race, war, and equality swept the country. Cities were set alight. Protestors were shot and killed. Civil Rights leaders and Presidents slain. It was a decade of turbulence characterized by youth questioning authority. At the same time, hippie communes began to emerge in California. Make peace not war. Grow Grass, not Hate were common refrains. The country was shocked to read about Charles Manson and his plan for a national race war called *Helter Skelter*. A young pregnant woman died, with her baby cut from her womb and grotesquely displayed. The USA was ablaze.

A cult will be critical of social systems and government. The cult will openly question social norms and power structures. As the secretive group gains control of its members, the followers also begin to preach the gospel. Don't trust the government. Your parents hate you. Everyone else is lost in the world...except for us! Trust us, follow us, listen to us, LOVE US! For we have the answers.

Manson Family

By most accounts, Charles Manson was a short, hippie loser. Not much to look at. Called 'Crazy Charlie' by ranch hands, Manson looked more like a hobo than a mass killer and psychopath. The product of a broken home and constant moving as a child, what Manson lacked in stability, he made up for with sheer darkness.

Some would call it charisma. Others would call it hypnosis or conditioning. Others still would call it Neuro-Linguistic Programing. Charlie appealed to a lost generation, because he had the answers. The majority of his followers came from America's middle-class. They were Sunday School teachers, daughters of business people, and children of wealthy families. Yet everyone in the Family lacked something. And Charlie was there to fill the gaps.

Through powers of manipulation, persuasion, and constant selfless acts, Manson's hold over his followers grew exponentially. When Dennis Wilson (of the Beach Boys) encountered Manson one night and asked if

Manson was going to harm him, Manson responded with a gentle, "No, I love you man," and instead kissed Wilson's feet. Manson also had an uncanny knack to key right in on his followers' insecurities. Manson would fill those gaps and give his family a feeling of wholeness. Charlie would offer his followers *unconditional love.*

The followers felt they were part of something important. Their lives now had meaning. They belonged. The followers left the past behind, started anew, and emerged with a true family. It is this dark vision of control and belonging that is seen again and again with cults.

A cult leader will separate his followers from society. The leader will then train and condition his followers to obey. The cult leader has all the answers. Every answer from the deepest question of your soul to the mysteries of the infinite universe. The cult leader will analyze you quickly, figure out what you lack, and then tailor the message to meet that need. It's almost as if you're at a car dealership, to buy new wheels, but have no idea what you want. The salesperson will then ask you questions, figure out what appeals to you, and provide you a car. Except instead of selling you a car, a cult leader steals your soul.

It is this targeted fulfillment of every need that brings followers in. The cult leader will have all the answers to life's deepest questions. We are taught to seek out the holy man at the top of the mountain. To search for the Buddha in the furthest cave. To explore the boundaries of our planet and discover the deepest secrets of the cosmos.

Yet, the cult leader will have all the answers already. Through a dark use of psychology, the cult leader will seduce you with knowledge, power, and awakening.

Peoples Temple of the Disciples of Christ – Jonestown

The Peoples Temple of the Disciples of Christ, known as the *Peoples Temple*, was a cult created by Jim Jones. Jones was a struggling preacher and communist in the 1950s, who decided to merge the two movements to create a force for social change that emphasized equality. Finding little early success, Jones constantly updated the message of his church to reach more and more followers.

Yet Jones was a dichotomy. He despised homosexuality, yet he openly took male and female lovers to give them what he called his 'spiritual energy'. Jones was an atheist and criticized the Bible as a book of lies, but then Jones would model his actions on the preaching of Jesus. Jones asked his followers to live a frugal and socially equal lifestyle. Yet Jones enjoyed the trappings of luxury that the millions of dollars from followers' donations provided - expensive suits, jewelry, private jets, and limousines.

Many followed Jones because of his speaking style. Jones would alternate thunderous crescendos with periods of silence. Jones and his followers also faked healings because the healings brought in additional money to the cult. The healings used chicken livers and animal organs to fool followers that Jones had magical powers to heal the sick by pulling out diseased organs from sickly patients. Jones also claimed clairvoyant abilities that brought in additional followers from the Spiritualist movement. Yet, the secret information that Jones knew about people (addresses, social security numbers, and phone numbers) was information obtained by private investigators.

In 1959, Jones started using his fiery sermon style and the *us versus them* message. As the Peoples Temple gained power, the temple required that members spend more and more time with 'Temple Family' and less time with blood relatives. During holidays such as Christmas, Thanksgiving, and Easter, the temple had mandatory gatherings. (Authors' note: This will be important later on with NXIVM). The temple elite wanted to break down blood ties strengthened by social customs and replace these ties with temple ideology.

Jones also began to subtly push his image as a Christ-like figure. Jones would embrace the image that he was a reincarnated Christ, espousing the message of a Christ consciousness and Christ-based revolution. Jones also took the role of messianic leader, preaching an upcoming doomsday of nuclear war.

Although the Temple preached social equality, its own structure included hierarchical levels of power and autocratic control. At the top of the Temple were the Temple Staff – a group of ten college educated women that undertook the highest priority missions for the Temple. At the top of the pyramid was Jones. He took advantage of his portrayal as a Christ and accepted the hero worship gladly. People inside the Temple were family. Anyone outside the group were enemies and traitors. Jones was also paranoid, insisting on traveling in an armored bus with machinegun-wielding bodyguards.

Through the use of social service organizations, and non-profits, Jones and the Temple beguiled and seduced major California politicians. These secular leaders included Jerry Brown, Harvey Milk, Walter Mondale, and Rosalynn Carter. Jones would help local communities with food drives, social improvement projects, and trash cleanup days. He would then use the local momentum and publicity to meet politicians and continue the charm offensive. During the height of Temple influence, Jones had many followers in the business community, government, and courts.

In 1977, due to increased scrutiny, Jones fled to the South American country of Guyana. He preached that the Temple would create a socialist paradise and heaven on earth. Over the next year, over a thousand followers left America to live with Jones in his new Guyanese settlement – known as Jonestown.

Alarmed at reports of sexual misconduct, slavery, and violence, the U.S. Congress launched a fact-finding mission to Jonestown in November 1978. The aftermath was shocking. As Congressman Leo Ryan attempted to leave Jonestown, he was shot and killed. Also killed were three journalists and one temple defector. On the night of November 18, 1978, knowing that additional U.S. forces would soon arrive, Jones began his final exit. Jim Jones ordered his followers to drink a mixture of grape-flavored Kool-Aid and cyanide. 918 people died that night, including 276 kids.

A cult will begin to assert control over its members by preaching an *us versus them* message. The cult will seek to dissolve family blood ties by arranging events over traditional social holidays. The cult leader welcomes comparisons to a Messiah or Christ. The cult structure will also be very hierarchical, with secret groups at the top and the cult leader at the apex. Admission into these secret groups occurs over stages, forcing members to spend more and more time with the cult in order to gain entrance to higher levels and secret knowledge.

The cult will also seek to gain acceptance in the local community by recruiting famous politicians and actors. The dark group will seek acceptance, and praise from national and international religious figures.

Branch Davidians – Waco

The Branch Davidians began as a breakaway sect of Seventh Day Adventists. The first Davidian was Benjamin Roden. Roden took over the Mount Caramel compound outside of Waco, Texas from a previous breakaway sect of Seventh Day Adventists called the *Shepherd's Rod* in 1959. The Davidians saw themselves as earthly representatives of Christ - the true *Branch* of the Root of David. The most famous Davidian was David Koresh

Koresh was born Vernon Howell in 1959 to a 14-year old single mother. His early childhood was lonely and sad. Due to dyslexia, Howell had to learn to memorize copious facts and written passages to keep up with other schoolchildren. Howell ended up dropping out of school and taking odd jobs to survive. After being thrown out of his local Seventh Day Adventist church, Howell moved to Waco in 1982 and joined the Branch Davidians.

While in Waco, Howell tried and failed in several business ventures. But, Howell found his niche at Mount Carmel (the Branch Davidian compound). Through his near photographic memory and recall of Bible stories, Howell emerged as a leader in the Branch Davidian sect. With striking good looks and a mesmerizing speaking style, Howell also found his way into the bed of sixty-year-old Lois Roden (the widow of Branch Davidian founder Benjamin Roden).

Lois was the last leader of the Branch Davidians prior to Howell's rise to power. Howell preached that he and Roden would birth the one true Messiah. After Lois Roden's death, a power struggle began between Roden's son George and Howell. Howell was kicked out of the Mount Carmel compound in 1985. However, Howell would return in 1989 when George Roden was arrested and convicted for the murder of Wayman Dale Adair. Roden was furious when Adair claimed he (Adair) was the true Messiah. Roden killed Adair with an axe blow to the skull.

In 1991, Howell traveled to California to recruit new followers for the Branch Davidians. Howell also changed his name to reflect his self-proclaimed combination of King David and King Cyrus (*Koresh* is the Biblical name of Persian King *Cyrus* the Great). Returning with additional followers and a new name, Koresh implemented his radical vision of biblical power. Koresh believed in and preached his messianic vision of worship through the 'Serpent's Root' and 'Seven Seals' teachings. David Koresh now claimed he was the manifestation of the lamb mentioned in the New Testament book of Revelation. The lamb, like John the Baptist, would presage the 2nd coming of Christ.

Koresh took advantage of his female followers, by claiming that he and they would birth a new lineage of saints and world rulers described in Revelation. Koresh's teachings gave him access to a harem of young women. And Koresh abused his power, by forcing his female followers to forgo any other type of sexual activity (except for sex with Koresh). Koresh also slept with girls as young as 12.

David Koresh's apocalyptic vision was made manifest on February 28, 1993 when United States ATF (Alcohol Tobacco Firearms & Explosives) agents raided the Branch Davidian compound at Mount Carmel. The ATF was concerned that the Branch Davidians were stockpiling automatic weapons and assault rifles, while crimes of child abuse of polygamy took place inside the compound. The initial assault on Mount Carmel was a disaster. Four ATF agents were killed, 16 agents were wounded (including one agent who shot himself in the leg), and numerous women and children were trapped in the compound.

The siege of the Branch Davidian compound reached its fiery finale on April 19, 1993 when the FBI began a final assault. Using an armored reconnaissance vehicle, the FBI pumped tear gas into the compound. Shortly thereafter, three simultaneous fires erupted in different parts of the building. The conclusion was, and still is, a shocking episode in American consciousness – 83 dead, including: women, children, and the charismatic David Koresh.

Heaven's Gate

Marshall Applewhite had several failed careers before settling into the role of a religious cult leader. Applewhite was well-versed in the Bible and taught at the University of Alabama (where he was fired for having a relationship with a male student) in 1965. Applewhite then went to teach at the University of St. Thomas in Houston, Texas, where later he quit due to a serious bout of depression in 1970. While hospitalized for depression in 1972, he met nurse Bonnie Nettles at a psychiatric ward.

Nettles and Applewhite both shared a passion for interpreting the Bible. Nettles also disclosed to Applewhite that both had been friends in a past life. After Applewhite's release, the pair became close as they formed a unique bond due to their fascination with the Bible and UFOs. The duo began to travel the country, preaching their radical brand of Bible Ufology and ancient astronaut theories. The pair believed that appearances of God or Angels in the Bible were really UFOs and extraterrestrials that the ancient Hebrews mistook for God.

Both also believed they were in direct contact with UFOs and had been given higher-level minds to interpret the Bible and guide humanity into a higher evolutionary state. Applewhite and Nettles began to preach the theory of 'Walk-Ins' to New Age conferences on the West Coast. They developed a following after presenting several workshops in California in 1975. Applewhite and Nettles called themselves 'The Two' or the 'UFO Two' and preached that they were the two witnesses prophesied of in the book of Revelation. The UFO Two were sent by divine beings to guide humanity during the end times. The teaching of The Two focused on salvation through individual growth, much like the self-help movement that came after the New Age era.

The pair soon began to call themselves 'Do' and 'Ti' (pronounced Doe and Ty). Do and Ti led their followers across the Rocky Mountains and Texas in the late 70s, living a nomadic lifestyle and staying on campgrounds. The two also increased their hold over followers by claiming they (Do and Ti) were divine messengers - the cult members were taught that only Do and Ti could receive spiritual messages from the higher level beings. The pair also insisted on strict obedience to their orders and loyalty from their followers (following the pair's orders without question, even though the orders might change).

To gain further control over the group, Do and Ti insisted that group members should limit contact with outsiders. Do also taught followers to be submissive - to act like pets or children in order to dissolve ego. This acceptance of authority to The Two would be the ultimate sign of devotion, while at the same time increasing the group members' dependency on their leaders. Members were encouraged to seek Do's advice on every issue. The cult members would describe Do as patient and fatherly.

The group gathered additional followers and more money in the early 1980s. The cult began to live together in a pod of houses, allowing access to one another during all times of day and night. In 1985, Nettles died. Do (Applewhite) began to preach that Nettles had evolved into a higher spiritual consciousness, and that Nettles was still communicating with him. Do also preached that Jesus was an extraterrestrial that was taken into a spaceship during the ascension. Since Jesus didn't find enough evolved souls on his first visit, it was now Do's role to prepare the way for Jesus's return.

Followers were taught that the only way to eternal salvation was through Do. Applewhite encouraged his devotees to view him as a Christ-like and Messianic figure. By following Do, the devotees could reach the 'Next Level' in evolutionary consciousness and travel to other planets to teach and convert others. Do also stated that alien intelligences could 'Walk-In' to his body to preach and relay messages. Do is said have combined elements of Christianity, technology, science fiction, and New Age mysticism. Applewhite also noted there were evil aliens called 'Luciferians' sent to destroy humanity and interfere with his divine mission.

From the mid-80s to the mid-90s, membership dwindled, then grew again after Applewhite paid for a full-page ad in USA Today. By the late 1990s, the group was gaining prominence again as it found a new source of income (building websites) and the cult began to call itself 'Higher Source.' The group recruited heavily from the internet. Higher Source then moved to a 9,000 square foot rented mansion in the exclusive San Diego County enclave of Rancho Santa Fe and began living communally.

Believing that his health was failing, and coinciding with the arrival of the Hale-Bopp comet, Do began his final prophecy. Do revealed to his followers that a UFO was trailing the Hale-Bopp comet and that his long-lost friend Ti was aboard the UFO. Do told his followers that Ti was ready to welcome them all to a new stage of evolution. But to get beamed aboard, the cult members had to discard their physical bodies and die, so that their spiritual souls could be released and beamed to the UFO.

Before consuming a fatal mixture of barbiturates and alcohol, Do recorded one final, chilling message. Appearing wild eyed, yet calm, Do told the world that the Heaven's Gate would only be open for a limited time and that the cult members were ready to pass through. After drinking the deadly cocktail, the cult members covered themselves with purple shrouds and settled in for a fatal and final rest. 38 members of the Heaven's Gate Cult were found dead on March 26, 1997. Two remaining Heaven's Gate members completed a suicide pact and killed themselves a year later.

The Secret of James Arthur Ray

In the mid-2000s, a publishing phenomenon and video spread like wildfire in the United States. 'The Secret' by Rhonda Byrne promised quick success. A person only needed to ask for, believe, and then receive anything under the sun. Not having success? Well, you just need to *visualize*. By visualizing the goal or item desired, it would manifest in your life.

The Secret was criticized as simplistic - a rehash of the Bible's Matthew 21:22 (And all things, whatsoever ye ask in prayer, believing, ye shall receive). Yet, the book was showcased on popular television talk shows including Oprah and Larry King Live. Adherents to the New Age book had mixed results. The book also promoted the New Thought movement - that God is Supreme, Infinite, and Everlasting; that Divinity can be found within each person; that the highest spiritual principal is loving one another unconditionally; and that our mental states manifest our experience. The ones that did find major monetary success with *The Secret* were writer Rhonda Byrne and the gurus featured on *The Secret* DVD. One such self-professed guru was James Arthur Ray.

Ray grew up in Tulsa, Oklahoma the son of a preacher. Ray would later claim that his family was dirt poor, yet childhood friends remember Ray was well-dressed and middle-class. Ray provides very little info about his upbringing, other than the myth of poverty and struggle.

But, Ray's father actually worked full-time at a Sears and his mother retired from American Airlines. Ray's parents owned a trailer park for additional income. Ray was known as a braggart in High School. After graduating, he became a professional bodybuilder, was married, divorced, and also started, then dropped out of Junior College. Ray's only steady employment was working sales with AT&T. Ray later claims he had a 'spiritual revelation' while taking the 'Boca Grande' (large mouth) of Ayahuasca in Peru. However, there is no such thing as a Boca Grande dose of Ayahuasca. Consuming a larger dose of Ayahuasca will not increase the vividness of your trip – it will only make you pass out. And there is no way to verify when or even if Ray ever traveled to Peru to consume the hallucinogen.

In the late 90s, Ray began marketing his New Age experience using AT&T sales techniques. In 2000, Ray launched seminars based on the law of attraction and the principles of ask, believe, receive. Ray quickly shot to the top of the New Thought guru circuit with exciting seminars that subjected followers to sleep deprivation, fasting, fire walking, glass walking, and sweat lodge ceremonies. Yet, the sweats were extremely dangerous as participants were forced to forgo water beforehand and then placed in enclosed tents with high temperatures. Ray's other controversial activities including dressing up his followers as homeless people (and asking them to compare the responses they received) and also ordering his followers to place arrow tips on their necks and lean into the arrows. Yet, Ray never seemed to actually participate in these dangerous challenges; instead only ordering his followers to partake.

James Arthur Ray's downfall began in 2009. He organized a sweat lodge ceremony outside of Sedona in Yavapai County, Arizona. The followers (who each paid $10,000 for the event) were put through several tests to awaken their so-called Inner Spiritual Warriors. The participants were first made to sleep in the Arizona desert with only a sleeping bag. The next day, they were taken to a buffet and only allowed to eat food. No water could be consumed. Shortly after, the group was taken to a sweat lodge (a heated tent) built by Ray and subjected to extreme temperatures.

While the participants were being roasted alive, Ray would come in and out, drink water, and encourage the group to stay strong, believe in themselves, and not give up. The outcome was tragic - 3 dead and countless injured. After talk surfaced of a criminal investigation, Ray fled the county and went into hiding. Ray turned himself in and was then charged and convicted of criminally negligent homicide. He was sentenced to two years in Arizona State prison.

Ray was criticized by Native American groups for cultural appropriation. His desire for fame and fortune came at the expense of his reputation and the lives of 3 human beings.

2 BEGINNINGS

I first met Allison Mack in Vancouver, Canada in 2009. I was going to the film editing bay to work with my friend Matt Lyons. I hired Matt's company, Radius Squared, to help me log footage and produce some demo reels for my film *Heaven in Exile.* I had just returned from a whirlwind tour of India, spending time with numerous Tibetan Buddhists including the His Holiness the Dalai Lama and the Karmapa. I also interviewed Tai Situ Rinpoche, the State Oracle of Tibet, and the young Kalu Rinpoche. It was an epic trip and gathering of Tibetan Buddhist All-Stars.

Radius Squared is owned by Kaleena Kiff and Galen Fletcher. I had just walked in and was going to the Final Cut workstation (Final Cut is the editing software we use) to sit down with Matt. I suddenly noticed a very attractive blonde woman standing in the corner of the room.

"Hey Omar, how's it going?" asked Matt.

"Good. What's up?" I replied

"This is Allison, Allison Mack."

Wow. I thought silently. She was very pretty! In the CW TV show *Smallville*, Allison plays Chloe Sullivan, the hapless sidekick to Tom Welling's young Superman. In the show, her character is dorky and the episodes don't really showcase her beauty. This was Allison? She was gorgeous and had piercing Blue eyes. Wow.

"Hey, I'm Allie." Said the starlet.

"Good to meet you. Matt's been helping me with my film."

"Oh, what's it about?" Asked Allie.

I responded with a quick spiel of my trip, spending time with Dalai Lama and Karmapa, and the journey to India. Allie pretended to be interested for a few seconds, then looked away with boredom. Okay. Sorry. Didn't mean to bother you with my death-defying trip to the Himalaya.

Kaleena Kiff walked in the room. After saying goodbye, Allison walked out. Matt told me they were finishing work on a project for Allison. The production company worked on Allison's short films. I had seen Galen set up a really sweet camera shot (taken on a swing set, with a counterbalanced camera) in one of Allie's films. Not too shabby!

Matt and I spent the next few weeks logging footage, editing scenes, and putting together previews and demo reels. I felt we really captured something special. When we completed a demo reel, I asked for a production meeting with Kaleena and Galen.

We showed Kaleena and Galen the reel, and patiently waited for feedback.

"It's all wrong!" Noted Kaleena. (Kaleena is a former child actor and was a line producer on Smallville). "You need to emphasize different points."

"Uh-huh, uh huh. Yep." Agreed Galen.

"I want to see more Buddhism, more movement, more flow," added Kaleena.

Okay. So, I wrote down the critiques, went through my footage, and began to plug in more effective scenes. A film can always be improved. Being a Director and Editor, is like an artist – your work of art is never quite finished.

I could definitely shoot some more B-roll. B-Roll is background footage or footage that is not part of the main storyline, but used to support the main story. B-roll is secondary or supplemental footage.

Well, I could show someone meditating in the forest or in a Buddhist Temple. There is a really amazing Buddhist temple in Richmond, BC (about 30 minutes outside Vancouver). Hmmm… there is also one last person to interview. There is a female Buddhist Master that lives in British Columbia, about 1 hour north of Vancouver. Why not kill 3 birds with one stone: get more footage, do one last interview, and fill in the gaps?

"Hey Kaleena. I was thinking…do you think Allison Mack or Kristin Kreuk would be willing to shoot some B-roll and maybe do one last interview?" I asked. It sounded like a good idea. Matt had mentioned that Radius Squared (their production company) also made short films for Kristin Kreuk and her new company *Girls by Design*.

Kaleena turned her head and looked straight at me.

"Allie may want to help. She's really cool about helping filmmakers and wanting to improve the planet." Responded Kaleena.

"You don't want to work with Kristin. She's in The Cult. Didn't you know?" Asked Kaleena.

I will never forget Kaleena's response, because she didn't say 'a cult,' or 'a religious group,' or 'she's really busy with her group.' Kaleena said…'The CULT'.

"You mean, the band?" I asked.

"No. Kristin's in a cult. She's totally brainwashed, everything she does is for the Cult. The leader is some creepy guy with a beard. Kristin worships a woman that calls herself Perfect." Responded Kaleena.

Whaaaaaaaat?

Did she just say that? How do you respond to that? What do you say, when someone flat out tells you that a person is in a cult?

I didn't know how to respond. So, I just said, "Okay."

It's pretty bad when your own employees and production company don't want to work with you, because they think you are a brainwashed cult member. I didn't believe it. I didn't want to believe it. At the time, Kreuk was playing the role of the ingenue - the innocent, wholesome character of Lana Lang on Smallville.

I thought to myself, 'Nah…can't be real. Who would believe that?' At home, I researched the topic on internet message boards. There was something about a group in New York. The leader liked to play volleyball and hear acapella. What? Nah, can't be real.

I put the episode out of my mind. Matt and I worked on polishing the demo reel and actually came up with a really good cut. It was in the can (sound locked, edited, ready to go) and we sent the new version to Kaleena and Galen.

'Looks good,' they responded. Cool. Back to editing.

****

Late that Spring, I was on my book tour. I was in the East Coast visiting bookstores and doing signings in Salem, Boston, Springfield, and New York promoting 'Elemental Shaman'. That was my first novel. The book is about journeys to Arizona, Guatemala, and Bhutan to meet spiritual masters and convey their messages. A mixture of travel guide and teachings from spiritual people.

When I was in Vancouver, BC, I asked my friends to recommend a webmaster. I was told Tabitha Chapman was good. Tabby is a kind soul and capable webmistress. We put together a site that looked like a world map. You could click on a part of the world and read a little blurb about that journey. I liked the look of the site – it was mysterious and sleek. Site was published. I was on my way.

Book sales were slow at first, but as each week passed, sales ramped up. I did a radio circuit, podcasts, and author events to build interest in Elemental Shaman. About the same time (in mid-April), I read that His Holiness the Dalai Lama was slated to visit Albany, NY for a speech but cancelled. That's kind of strange. Why would the Dalai Lama cancel a speech?

I have always been fortunate to wind up in front of the Dalai Lama whenever I see him. Always by accident, always through a weird series of events. Once in McLeod

Ganj, India, I would up right at his feet. Because I was
sitting with legs crossed in the room. But, behind me was
an Indian woman (the wife of a senior diplomat) and she
started yelling at me. She wanted to stretch her legs out
(even though everyone else was sitting cross-legged), so
she scolded me and demanded that I move. The space
was so small, there was nowhere else to go. So, I ended
up sitting on the wooden steps, right at the foot of the
Dalai Lama's throne. Not a problem. That's pretty cool
for me.

Back in New York, I opened my laptop and started
reading articles in the Albany Sun Times – the local
newspaper that reported on the event. The Dalai Lama
cancelled his speech in Albany because questions were
raised about the sponsors. The name of the group
sponsoring the lecture was NXIVM (pronounced
Nexium, nex-eee-um). Supposedly the group was a cult
and the leader was some guy named Keith. Well, that
doesn't sound like a name for a Cult leader. Not a very
impressive cult anyways. But, to his followers, he was
'the Vanguard'.

So, his followers called him Vanguard. Okay, but
how is that a cult? Just because someone has a nickname,
doesn't mean they are a Cult Leader. In Law School, I
had a professor – Guy Wellborn. He would tell us stories
in torts class about his buddies. And all his pals had
nicknames. There was Tiny – he was a 400lb guy,
nicknamed in contrast to his size. Killer – who had killed
a burglar that was running away (Killer told the police
that he had aimed high with his shotgun, and missed, but
really didn't). And Looney Tunes – because…you

guessed it, he had been locked up in the State mental ward.

So, a nickname does not a cult leader make. Right? RIGHT???

I decided to investigate. I began reading up on the subject. I researched Jonestown, Heaven's Gate, Scientology. Some of the stuff is pretty damn weird. One of the alleged tenets of Scientology is that the Earth was populated 5 million years ago by a Warrior Priest named *Xenu* who brought his followers along in spaceships, yet killed them all with hydrogen bombs. The spirits of the followers (called Thetans) now attach themselves to humans and have caused havoc for millions of years. Problems with diabetes? It's not the Krispy Kremes you're sucking down like cold water on a blazing day. Blame it on the Thetans. But, you only find this out after paying $1 Million dollars for Scientology classes. What the heck?!?!?! Allegedly, that is.

But, why would a cult be in Albany, New York? I like upstate New York and the Catskills as much as the next person…but why not Hawaii? Or take the traditional route, and go full mountain-man style in Colorado or Utah? Right?

Sure enough, within a week, the Albany Sun Times noted that the event was back on and scheduled for May 6, 2008. The Dalai Lama was coming to Albany! Perfect chance to see his Holiness again and figure this shit out. Right at the end of my book tour. Good timing, great. So,

who was this monster that everyone was scared of?
Surely, no monsters are named Keith…or are they?

3 THE MONSTER

I checked into the Albany Fairfield Inn on Wednesday night. As the cool breeze of the evening filled my room, I was lost in thought. I undressed, hit the shower, and let the warm droplets of water dance and run along my body.

The origins of cults can probably be traced back to our tribal ancestors. When human beings first walked on the Earth some 200,000 years ago, working together in bands was necessary for survival. Not everyone could hunt, not everyone could plant. Leaders emerged to guide the wanderers across the landscape. And questions remained.

Mysterious things happened. Why did the sun rise everyday? How is it that you could see the sun, and walk towards it, but never touch it? And what about the mysterious white ball, the glorious moon rising almost every evening. Why would it change shape?

First no moon, then a waxing moon, growing larger each evening. Until a full moon filled the Earth with its pale blue and gentle light. Who made the mountains? The skies, the wind? Surely the gods. But who knew the Gods? Was it the shamans, with their dances and painted skin? Or was it the leaders and tribal chiefs? Who knew the will of the Gods and could explain their whims and desires?

Cult leaders take advantage of followers by claiming to have all the answers. We all have questions. It is part of the human experience to have questions and seek answers. These are the same questions we've asked for 250,000 years. Why are we here? What happens when we die? How do find meaning, in seemingly meaningless lives? In an infinite universe, do we really matter?

By claiming to have all the answers, cult leaders take advantage of human frailty and the inquisitive nature of our species. Yet beware traveler…if you see the Buddha in the middle of the Road with all of life's questions explained – Kill them!

The next day, I arrived at the venue about 20 minutes early. The Dalai Lama was appearing at the Albany Palace Theater. It seems every large city has either a Paramount or Palace. Go to the palace to see the guru. Climb to receive the paramount (most important) answers. From the start something seemed off.

I've been to several lectures and teachings from His Holiness – from Wisconsin, to Seattle, to India. Every time, there's always a large crowd in the building. This time, there were people, but no one was in the front.

Everyone was sitting anxiously in the back. The front was almost totally empty. Weird!

The only thing in the front was a small, roped-off section of seats. I sat down behind these empty seats, on the right side of the theater. Also conspicuously absent, was His Holiness's throne. Usually when the Dalai Lama gives teachings, he will sit upon his throne or a version of it. I have seen the larger throne (almost 12 feet tall). I have seen the smaller throne (about 7 feet tall). But this time, no throne. Instead there were a few seats, two on one side and about 5 on the other, both facing the audience. To the left of the stage was the setup for a band. Several microphones and music stands were up. No real activity towards the front. A large group of people was seated in the back of the theater. And me, right in the middle of the void.

After a few minutes a band walked in. They grabbed instruments, sheet music, and started to play. Nothing spectacular, just some intro vanilla pop. Soon more people began to emerge from the front. Then a larger group came in wearing white scarves. Before I knew it, the front section was packed. Yet, the middle was still empty. And more people were seated towards the back.

His Holiness arrived. The Dalai Lama sat down with his translator. The group with white sashes took their seats within the reserved section. A couple of members with white sashes sat on the stage, to the right of the Dalai Lama. In the reserved seats group was a tall man, wearing a Khaki shirt and trousers and an outback-style hat. That's kinda weird – we're not on Safari. Why are you wearing a hat indoors, Crocodile Dundee?

The Dalai Lama gave his speech on compassion. Nothing noteworthy. I do remember one line - his Holiness spoke about ethics. And how if one had indeed committed an ethical breach, they should admit it. About the same time, I noticed a cute blonde woman amongst the group with the reserved seats. I know that profile! The attractive features, good hair. It was Allison! Allie Mack.

His Holiness kept speaking about improving the world, working on one's karma, escaping samsara (the endless cycle of birth, death, and rebirth due to karma). During the speech, Allie kept looking back at me. She would look back at me a few times and make quizzical faces. Like, 'Don't I know you?' or 'You look familiar'.

As His Holiness finished the speech, a man emerged from stage left. He was dressed head to toe in black, wore thin-rimmed glasses, and had a salt-pepper beard. He slowly walked up to His Holiness, and presented his Holiness a white sash. The Dalai Lama then took the sash and placed the sash around the bespectacled man's neck. The man thanked his Holiness and moved off stage.

A very shy and soft-spoken woman then went to the podium. At the end of each public teaching, the organizers of events for the Dalai Lama announce the financial report. So-and-so many dollars made for tickets, such-and-such was the cost of the event. Any excess went to His Holiness's charities and the Tibetan

Government-in-Exile. After the shy blonde woman gave the figures, there was a collective gasp – the event had lost money! Almost $300,000 was lost. Ouch. Ticket sales were just not there.

The event ended and I walked amongst the groups in the front. I went up to Allison.

"Hey Allie, how's it going? Congratulations." I said.

"I remember you…you're from the…" she said as her voice trailed.

"From Vancouver. Kaleena and Galen were helping me edit my film." I said.

"Right." She replied. "How's your film going?"

"Really good. I'm on my book tour right now." I said.

We talked for a few more moments. Allie was kind, cheerful, and pleasant. Piercing blue eyes. A simple compassion radiated from her. That is the Allie Mack I knew. I said my goodbyes and kept walking around.

Someone nearby called Crocodile Dundee by name.

"Mark. Mark Vicente! What are you doing here?" The person asked. So, that was the tall dude. Kind of dressed out-of-place for a teaching from the Dalai Lama. Still wearing his hat, indoors. But, it's America. Wear what you want.

I didn't want to listen to the conversation, so I kept walking. I made my way to the opposite side of where I was sitting – the left side of the auditorium. I noticed the diminutive man again, the one with glasses. The same man who was just on stage. The lilliputian fellow that was wearing all black. He was well-groomed with a salt and pepper beard.

I did notice he looked spaced out. Not like drugs spaced out, but like thousand-yard-stare spaced out. Glazed eyes. Like there, but not really. Strange.

Behind him, were also about 10 men in cheap and not-so-cheap suits. They looked pudgy, with short-hair, dark suits, white shirts, and maroon and blue ties. These must be attorneys. I walked up to the monster.

"You must be Keith." I asked. I read his full name the night before: Keith Alan Raniere (pronounced rain-ear-ee). Cult leader extraordinaire. He seemed quite ordinary actually. Like a hippie-wannabe, computer programmer.

"Yep. That's me." Replied the glassy-eyed guru.

"Everything turned out really well. Good job." Why did I say this? I'm really not sure. I guess I was nervous at the time. "How did you enjoy meeting the Dali Lama?" I asked

"Yeah, thanks." Responded Vanguard. "It was good." As the words rolled out of his mouth, I noticed he still had a glazed look upon his face.

This was the monster? The person everyone was so afraid of? He seemed very plain for a grand villain. I was expecting a werewolf. Instead, I ran into a computer nerd.

It didn't seem real. Keith was demure and milquetoast. Not quite exciting enough to make anyone's heart race. He seemed more like a boring Bill Gates than anything else. I then stepped back and sized up the sharks.

There was one attorney that caught my eye. He kept fiddling with something in his mouth. It was kind of distracting.

"How's it going?" I asked. It will surprise you how much personal information people reveal, if you just ask...

"Not so good. My tooth fell out. But I put it back it. I need to go to the dentist."

As he was saying this, he kept popping a molar out of his mouth, then back in his mouth. Out of his mouth, then back in. I noticed his thumb and forefinger had a gooey, reddish substance on it. Glad I didn't shake his hand. It was kind of gross.

"Yeah, you should really get that looked at." I didn't know what to say. What do you tell a grown man that keeps popping a molar in and out of his jaw? I slowly excused myself. As I was walking out of the theater, I notice Tabby. Tabitha Chapman, my web designer, was at the event.

I walked over and said Hello. Tabby mentioned how she was excited to meet the Dalai Lama. We exchanged the usual small talk – how are you, what are you up to, what do you have planned for later on today. I said goodbye and walked out.

I thought that was the last time I would ever meet the monster. Boy, was I wrong...

4 INVITATION

Months passed. The book tour went well. I was working on a final edit of my film Heaven in Exile. Around November, I received an email from Tabby. She wanted to talk to me about something important…

"Hey Omar, how are you?" Asked Tabby.

"Not bad, how's it going?" I responded

"Well hey, I have a really good opportunity for you to meet some people." Noted Tabby. "Great chance to make some connections, get the word out on your film."

"Sounds great. Tell me more." I responded.

Tabby replied that she knew I wanted to meet Allie Mack and Kristin Kreuk. So Tabby said I should take a course in Albany so that the group would get to know me better. Thinking back, that doesn't make a lot of sense. If you are working in Vancouver, why would you go to

Albany, New York to meet people, so you can return to Vancouver and meet someone already there?

"Well, if you meet these people, everyone will get to know you better. That way, you can meet who you want to meet." She explained.

"Okay." I noted.

Tabby said that the group had some negative press and not to believe the local newspaper. I said not a problem. Everyone should be given the benefit of the doubt. I'm fairly opened-minded. Besides, I already met Keith – the infamous Vanguard. And he didn't look like he could guard anything, except maybe a candle in a meditation center.

I agreed to take the classes. I gave Tabby my credit card info. The classes were not cheap – about $5,000 for a five-day intensive. And I needed to arrange my own transport and lodging. I remember Tabby said some of the group members rented out rooms in their homes. I asked Tabby if she could hook me up. Not a problem she said. She had the perfect person. I could stay with Ginger. Okay, sounds good!

Three weeks later, I was on a Southwest flight to Albany. I was stuck on the tarmac in Manchester, New Hampshire. The below-freezing temperatures and steady snow delayed all flights. I remember the ground crew first spraying the plane with a clear liquid. Then the deicing fluid covered my window in a light green shade.

Cults obtain their power over followers by coloring the outside world in distorted hues. Everyone is lost, everyone is confused except for cult members. Don't criticize the guru, they have all the answers. The outsiders are wrong. They have been tricked by parents, government, the devil, etc. The outsiders are parasites and subversives. They drain your life energy and your soul. Don't let them fool you...

Believe in us. Worship us! Follow us. For we're your new family. And we can show you God's true vision. We have the keys to humanity's future.

Don't believe in God you say? Well, don't worry. See, it's not really a God at all. It's really a super intelligence. An artificial intelligence, billions of years old, created the cosmos, stars, and planets. From whales to plankton, all of life exists by design. It's all a computer program, written and hidden in our DNA. See, we have unlocked the secrets and mysteries of life.

They're ready for you. And you're ready too! You're among the chosen. The special few human beings who can accept and process the great mystery.

Join us. We've been waiting for you. Dontcha know?

5 ARRIVAL

Tabby picked me up at the Albany airport. We made some small talk, nothing major. She was excited that I was taking the course. The five-day intensive was one of the best experiences of her life. Or so she said. I would meet the group. And soon, the person at the center of it all – the Vanguard.

Tabby had given a copy of my book *Elemental Shaman* to Nancy Salzman to read. I was screened so that my books would not copy the teachings of ESP. Tabby said I could not compete with NXIVM later on and reveal Vanguard's secrets to the world. How prophetic.

"But don't call her 'Nancy'. Her name is 'Prefect'." Said Tabby.

"You mean 'Perfect?'" I asked.

"It's PREFECT." Tabby answered quickly.

Ummm….okay. Prefect is an old English word. It

means senior student or magistrate. Head of the prefecture. Prefect. I had to look it up.

"ESP? So, does ESP stand for extra-sensory perception?" I asked.

"Nope. ESP is our Executive Success Program." Responded Tabby.

ESP was the Executive Success Program I was taking. It was created under the umbrella of NXIVM. NXIVM doesn't really stand for anything (or at least that's what Tabby said). In Latin, the letters sound close to *nexum,* which means 'connection'.

I would soon be an ESPian, noted Tabby. How exciting! How exciting indeed.

6 MOUTH

Tabby drove me to an office complex. We arrived at 455 New Karner Road, Albany, New York. The complex is called *Karner Woods*. It was a nice series of buildings: one-story, brown brick, brown roof, tinted windows, with a freshly re-paved parking lot. There was a parking space marked for 'L. Salzman'. But something was strange. Looking around, there were no other offices. Usually, in these types of office parks you see an accountant, attorney, a State Farm insurance office. But here, nothing. The only tenant was Executive Success Programs and the rest of the complex was unused.

Tabby parked and I walked towards the entrance. There was one door in, one door out. On the single glass door was a painted graphic that said 'Executive Success Programs'. On the panel to the right of the door, was some Chinese calligraphy.

I walked in. There was a long hallway, past the front door. The interior was various shades of brown and opened up to an atrium. To the right was another set of doors, leading to the classroom. The atrium opened up on the left side and had bench seating on the far wall. To the left of the seats was another classroom.

I met the trainer. She was wearing a silky orange sash over her clothes. Her name was Christine.

"Hello Omar. How are you?" She asked.

"Good good. Pleased to meetcha." I said.

Christine was an attractive lady, late 30s. She looked Irish – Jet black curly hair, shoulder length, fair skin, and piercing blue eyes. The bright orange sash hung loosely over her white pullover sweater. She began to speak to Tabby.

Eager to start, I walked towards the classroom on the right where the group was half a day into their five-day intensive. Christine quickly pulled me out and ushered me to the smaller classroom on the left side of the atrium. I had to start at the beginning. The lessons could be taught by the trainer, or could be watched on video. Christine started the video. I sat down.

"Hello. My name is Nancy Salzman. Call me Prefect." drolled the tv.

I sat through 3 hours of Nancy Salzman introducing herself and her prize mentor, Vanguard. Nancy never called Keith 'Keith'. It was always Vanguard. In the videos, she came across as smug and high strung. Kind of like a High School teacher, that seemed to know everything, but never left the Springfield city limits. There's a Springfield in every state, you know.

Nancy is not charismatic. On her presentation style, I would describe it as Ben Stein from *Ferris Bueller's Day Off,* but with just a dash of spice. Not a lot, just a little. Imagine sitting through 3 hours of Ben Stein talking. Nancy's voice was almost hypnotic. She spoke in the same dry tone, over and over. I swear I nodded off a few times. It was a lot of material.

Cults begin to convert their followers through prolonged programming and indoctrination. By constantly preaching the message, the followers' barriers break. Each of us has lines we will not cross, things we will not do. Or do we? Psychologists call it *Stockholm Syndrome*. After hours and hours of lecture, diatribe, and indoctrination – hostages will begin to identify with their captors. Some even take up arms. Would I find myself holding an AK and waving it around a bank? Or would the mind warp be a bust?

After three hours, Christine was ready to put me back in class. I had caught up with the rest of the newbies. Walking in the classroom, I was given the instructions:

"Okay, now before we enter, we always bow to Vanguard and thank him for his teachings." Noted Christine.

"Uhhhh…okay." I responded.

Christine then walked me to the classroom door. She bowed towards Vanguard's picture at the far wall. Clapped her hands once, loudly. And said,

"Thank you Vanguard!"

I did it too! It seemed kinda silly, but why not? I paid for the class right? I might as well get the full experience. After the salutation, I went to an open chair in a row of tables. The rest of the class was just on a break. It was about 5pm. We were just about to start another session.

The way the classes are taught is fairly straightforward. The instructor will show a video of Nancy Salzman talking for about 50 minutes. In it, Nancy smiles her Nancysmile, while she gives a presentation about the lessons of ESP. Her voice is always the same tone. It is like a smug, matter-of-factly, 'Okay Boys and Girls, we are going to sharpen our pencils today.' And on, and on.

After the lesson, the class is then broken up into groups. There are two to three coaches, one per group. The coaches then pull out flashcards and ask the group to work out morally confusing scenarios.

Is it ethical to kill a baby to save 10 humans? What about 1000 humans?

Is it acceptable to lie, to maintain your values?

What is worse, murder or lying?

If you kill a homeless person, is this really a bad thing if it means the rest of humanity has more food?

The kicker is that there are no answers to these questions (I did not find this out, until the end of the course when one of the coaches slipped and showed me the cards). The purpose of these questions is two-fold: 1) break down your psychological and moral barriers, 2) convince you that ESP is the superior framework to make decisions.

We all have a moral compass. Lessons we grew up with. Teachings from parents, schools, principals, church, TV, etc. Don't steal. Don't lie. Murder is wrong. Kill only in self-defense, if at all. These morals are programmed into our psyche through lessons and a risk/reward framework. Do great in school, get a good job. Obey the law, stay out of jail. Break the law, go into prison. If you can't do the time don't do the crime. But, what if someone could delete your moral programming and replace it?

What if someone teaches you that not paying income taxes is perfectly okay? That murder, to save the lives of others, is fine? That homeless people are to blame for their own suffering. There are no victims in life, dontcha know? Homeless people are homeless because they are lazy. And charity groups are just as corrupt. So, why even donate? Instead, give your money and time to NXIVM. This is what the flashcard scenarios are built to do – make you question your entire belief system through nonsense scenarios.

Thinking about it now, it really is dark and insidious. Through these questions, you are convinced by a group that it is: 1) okay to murder, 2) acceptable to steal, and 3) that everyone outside the group is a parasite. And the 'group think' begins to turn members of the group who have doubts. And reinforces members that have accepted the lessons. It's basically hypnosis through group think and peer pressure. Subconsciously, we all want to feel acceptance and fit in. Do this in a controlled environment, and you can convince students of almost anything.

We finished the module, then had our dinner in the atrium. Christine had setup the food: bagels, fruit, and veggies. No meat. No coffee. Just a spartan meal. We did a couple more sessions that night before being released at 9pm. Get some rest, Christine noted. Back at 7am the next day to start!

I was given a ride to my lodgings. I asked to stay with the group, I wanted to find out more about these people. After a few miles, we arrived in a nice middle-class neighborhood. I would be staying at a White two-story house. My caretaker and owner of the house was a woman named Ginger.

You ever see those retired ladies playing Bingo? Early 60s, with the big hoop earrings? Heavy smoker, a bit loud and obnoxious. That was Ginger, to a 'T'.

I walked in the house. The foyer led to a kitchen. Ginger told me more about herself. She had known Nancy Salzman. Whoops… 'Prefect'. She had known 'Prefect' for almost 20 years, back when 'Prefect' was just an RN. As she kept talking in her raspy, smoker's voice, hoop earrings jingling, I noticed a picture on her refrigerator. It was on a calendar. At first, I thought it was Jesus. Hell, it looked like Jesus.

There was this wispy-eyed, bearded man with his headed tilted up, palms folded, locked in some faraway gaze. But it wasn't Jesus.

"Hey Ginger, who's that?" I asked.

"That's Vanguard. Our Vanguard. You know, the Buddhists talk about a messiah arriving at the end of our age, to usher in a new era of peace. That's who Vanguard is." She noted.

She said this without missing a beat. Utterly convinced of this truth. Just in a matter-of-fact kind of way, like… 'Oh yeah, the Mets suck this year' or 'KFed is asking for more spousal support from Brittany' or 'Such and such judge got caught sniffing panties again.' Like it was utterly normal.

And it was kind of bizarre. As she was saying this, she also had a glazed look across her face. Thousand-yard stare. Up for long hours. Very little sleep. Your mind trying to process things, but not really. Like an automaton.

I knew what it looked like. I had seen it before in Marine Corps Officer Candidate School. I had seen it before in Law School. Someone that was there, but not really. Someone that was just exhausted, tired to the bones, repeating some words like a stuck CD. I tried to snap her out it. Shit, I tried to snap myself out of it.

"So Ginger. Nice house, how long have you been here?" I asked.

"Thanks. I like it." She said. "Lemme show you to your room."

I followed Ginger as she led me to the basement. It was setup in a dormitory-style layout. She had partitioned off the rooms with portable walls. The kind you see in grade school, where the walls have a blue-gray fabric cover and you post pictures with push-pins. Ginger would be sleeping in another portion of the room. I was assigned an area with two cots. Ginger excused herself for bed.

Yes, you read that correctly. Ginger owned the house for years, yet she slept in the basement so that other NXIVMs (Nexians) could sleep in her master bedroom. Kinda weird. If I owned a house, you wouldn't find me sleeping the basement.

I unpacked my belongings and was ready to hit the sack. About that time, there was a commotion upstairs. Heavy footfalls broke the silence, then were gone.

"Must be the Dogs!" Said Ginger.

I thought…'Huh?' I didn't see any dog bowls in the kitchen. Does she have some Golden retrievers? A Malamute?

As I drifted to sleep, I kept having the same nightmare. I was in a car, driving on a big interstate, driving the wrong way against a rush of cars. Barely missing car after car, avoid head-on collisions.

7 WALK

I woke the next morning at 6am. Showered, hopped in a car, and ready to go at 455 *Karner Woods* by 7am. Breakfast was a plain bagel and fruit. No butter, no jelly. No raisins. No coffee. Just bagels and fruit.

I took time to study the group. We had a Supreme Court Justice from Guatemala and his two sons. There was also a cute, thin blonde. And a couple of university grads. The coaches were Javier (from Mexico) and his girlfriend Ariella (from Canada). Before starting, I heard Javier (Javi for short) mention that he was going to have to marry someone to stay in the United States. He couldn't marry Ariella because she was Canadian and *she* needed to marry a U.S. Citizen if she wanted to stay in the USA. I thought they were joking. Apparently not.

We took our seats and began our daily programming from Nancy Salzman. Nancy would speak in the same voice. I would swear she was trying to hypnotize me. After she finished, we would sit around in small groups and discuss the nonsense scenarios from the flashcards.

Is it okay to lie, if you save someone's life? Do governments lie to us? If a government routinely lies, then is it ethical? If a government is built on lies, it is okay to overthrow that government?

A cult brainwashes members by using five basic principles. I call it IISAG. It stands for:

1) Isolate – remove new members from family and social groups

2) Indoctrinate – teach the same lessons again and again

3) Starve – reduce caloric intake

4) Attack morals – attack the newbie's old way of thinking, limits, morals, moral compass, and standards

5) Group think – introduce new thinking in small groups, so the newbie feels left out and must adopt the group norms

It is a very powerful and simple technique. Very effective. Will probably work on 97% of the population. And you can tell yourself, 'Oh…this would NEVER happen to me.' Wrong Halloween breath. Because it is so subtle, you wouldn't even know it's happening.

The basic principles of NXIVM and ESP can be reduced to 2 concepts: self-interest and moral relativism. That is, the highest and most important interest of the individual IS the individual. And that morals and morality do not exist, except in social groups. Thereby, if you combine the two concepts, you have a recipe to dominate the world.

And the Nexians are not shy about this. They proudly proclaim it's the duty of each member to obtain and control as much of the world's wealth and resources as possible. Wealthy members, such as the Seagram's heiresses, also give tons of money to state and national politicians including both Republicans and Democrats in New York state, the Clinton Foundation, and Hillary Clinton's campaign. Many argue this is why NXIVM was able to stay out of the spotlight for so long despite the numerous complaints to law enforcement. Money opens a lot of doors. Big Money owns state capitols.

Another lesson is that ESP and Nexians should not give to charity or be charitable. There are no victims in life – the downtrodden are suffering because of their own actions. Thereby, you should not waste your money or time in helping them – they deserve their circumstances.

Also, how can it be moral to give time or money to a corrupt charity, business, or government? If the government is going to waste your money, why pay taxes? If a charity is not giving 100% of the money collected to the homeless, why should you give it your money? The charity is inefficient. Don't volunteer at soup kitchens or with neighborhood cleanups. Your time is better spent making more money. And don't worry about the poor. The poor are suffering because of their own choices – so you should not be helping them to begin with, or you become an enabler.

Does that sound like a program that would be endorsed by the Dalai Lama? Don't give to the poor because they are lazy. Don't feed the homeless because they deserve to be on the street and dead in ditches.

Well guess what? NXIVM isn't endorsed by the Dalai Lama. When the Dalai Lama made his appearance in Albany, His Holiness came to speak to the *community* at the request of NXIVM. His Holiness did not speak exclusively to NXIVM. And his Holiness never endorsed NXIVM as a valid charity, group, or ethical foundation. Interesting, huh? Yet the Nexians will never put this on their website. Instead they proclaim, 'The Dalai Lama endorsed us. So we are good! Come be good with us!' Bullshit. Don't fall for it.

After five hours of teachings, we broke for lunch. Christine had set up some bagels, fruit, carrots, celery, and hummus for us to eat. Oh my! Not.

Thirty minutes later, we started again. I felt like taking a nap. Needed a break. Hard to go on. Felt really tired. Didn't want to go on. But no...back to it.

****

Before each class starts, and at the end of each day of instruction, the group forms in a circle and recites the following affirmations:

1) Success is an interior state of clear and honest awareness of who I am, my value in the world and my responsibility for the reactions I have to all things.

2) There are no ultimate victims; Therefore, I will not choose to be a victim.

3) I am committed to my success. I understand that we must all elevate ourselves – and thus elevate all others – just as everyone else elevates us. This is interdependence.

4) The success obtained by my own means is successfully gained. True success can not be stolen, copied or obtained by chance. I will not appear to be successful by these means or by any other. I will earn my own success.

5) Tribute is a form of payment and honor. It is an honor to honor those who merit it. I will use the tribute to praise others beyond my petty dislikes and dislikes. As a result, I will define my being and my true contribution to humanity.

6) Successful people do not steal and have no desire or need to steal. I will not steal anything. I will always earn what I need and want. Copying without permission or tribute is not a compliment, it is a robbery. The robbery is to take or receive anything without having earned it; it is always at the expense, however small, of others.

7) Inner honesty and integrity are the highest human values, and the foundation of human psychology. All other values emerge from them. I will never change my inner integrity or honesty for any other value.

8) The methods and information I learn in ESP are for my personal use only. I will not speak of them nor will I give to others knowledge of them outside ESP. Part of being accepted into ESP is to keep all the information confidential. If I violate this commitment, I am breaking a promise and breaching my contract, but more, I am deteriorating my internal and integrated honesty.

9) Real success is never at the expense of others. As a successful individual, I will never envy someone else's success. I will rejoice because I understand that the success of others elevates me, even a little, because I am also part of the human team. The updating of human potential by anyone is a tribute to the whole human team. If others are successful, I will protect their success against those who envy them. I promise to free myself from all habits that are based on parasitism and envy, and replace them with habits of effort and interdependence.

10) I will accept without reservation the success I have gained. I will accept neither more nor less. This is to accept with integrity. I will give unreservedly to those who have earned it. This is to give with integrity. I will accept with integrity as easily as I give with integrity. Not to accept what I am worth, or what I have won, is to devalue myself and, therefore, to

devalue all others.

11) People control the money, wealth and resources of the world. It is essential for the survival of humanity that these things are in control of successful and ethical people. I promise to ethically control as much money, wealth and resources of the world as possible within my plan of success. I will always support the ethical control of these things.

12) A world of successful people will undoubtedly be a better world; a world free from hunger, theft, dishonesty, envy and insecurity. People will no longer try to destroy each other, steal from each other, lower each other or rejoice at the loss of another. Success, ethics and integrity go hand in hand. I promise to share and enroll people in ESP and their mission for my own benefit and to make the world a better place to live

THANK YOU VANGUARD!!!

Reading the tenets again, they sound shocking. But again, we were exposed to hours and hours of lecture. And then our moral walls are broken down in the group session. To disguise the techniques, NXIVM loves to use peaceful sounding and innocent language. It's almost as if Nancy Salzman and Keith are obsessed with conveying an image of saccharine positivity. The cult uses names like: Rainbow Cultural Garden, World Ethical Foundation, Acapella Innovations to disguise their true intent.

And the explanation for NXIVM technology (most of it stolen from Scientology and Tony Robbins) is a word salad – a bunch of words, spoken together, that don't mean anything. The word salad is a hallmark of NXIVM and cults. Here is the NXIVM explanation for rational analysis, also known by the Nexians as 'Rational Inquiry':

Rational Inquiry® is a unique, patent-pending technology and body of knowledge created by scientist and mathematician, philosopher and entrepreneur Keith Raniere. It is based on the belief the more consistent an individual's beliefs and behavior patterns are, the more successful the person will be, and the greater his or her capacity of joy.

Rational Inquiry® is the technology behind NXIVM and is imparted by Executive Success Programs, Inc. and its President, Nancy Salzman. The model allows for the re-examination and integration of perceptions that may be the foundation of self-imposed limitations. It is also a tool for creating consistency in our language and removing errors of cognition. In this regard, it allows for the creation of permanent improvement and change. This technology yields reproducible, predictable and measureable results, and has a more personal application inspiring the individual to joyfully expand and grow.

Rational Inquiry® is more than a philosophy, it is a tool to create or examine philosophy—a process of philosophical development. In this sense, it assists

individuals to maximize their potential, gain a deeper understanding of ethics, develop critical thinking skills and the use of logic, and develop a deep and compassionate understanding of humanity. This method of ethical analysis, representing a new toolset for the system of human thought, has been cited as a discovery of historical proportions.

We invite you to experience what many are calling the most revolutionary discovery of our untapped potential.

What the hell does that mean? I don't even know. This is nonsense talk. It is several paragraphs that don't mean anything at all. Some call it gobbledygook. I call it word salad. It is a way of using fancy sounding words, and speaking in circles, that doesn't convey any meaning.

The lessons continued that day. Every now and then, our proctor Christine would pause and say tidbits about Vanguard's supernatural abilities.

"You know, if he meets you once, he will know who you are and remember your name forever." said Christine. That sounded cool, I thought.

She added, "Vanguard just plays his little heart out on the piano. The music is beautiful."

"He can tell your complete personality just by playing volleyball with you." Noted Christine.

With more and more classes, I felt like my emotional center was dwindling.

8 VEIL

We finished classes at 9pm. I hitched a ride back to Ginger's house. The door was unlocked, I walked right in.

Ginger was gone, but I found one of the 'dogs'. A group of ESPians was hanging out and talking. I sat down near the TV. There was a young man playing a video game. He was bald, lean, but he had the same glazed look in his eyes. I will never forget the conversation.

I introduced myself and it turned out 'Ben' was a former Marine Captain also. He had graduated The Basic School (Marine Officer Training) in the class before mine – Charlie Company in 1997. I was in Dirty Delta – the Best of the Best. I don't remember the tagline for Charlie Company. I don't think Ben even remembered.

He told me about getting dropped from Naval Flight School. In the Marine Officer Corps, we call these Marines 'fallen angels'. It's not necessarily a bad thing – not everyone can complete the flight training and medical requirements. These officers are transitioned into other MOSs (Military Occupational Specialties) so they can finish out their 4-to-6 year commitments. Some quit at the end of the 4. Some make the Marines a career. Still, it sucks when you fail a lifelong goal. So, was Ben looking for something in this colony of drifters, in this knot of lost souls?

Ben learned to fly and was working as a bush pilot in Alaska. But, a few hairy landings and a crashed plane ruined his career. Then he took NXIVM and ESP classes and was here. In Albany, New York – with a glazed look in his eyes, playing video games. I asked him what he had planned. He couldn't answer.

He did say that Nancy Salzman figured out a new business for him. He was unemployed, but Prefect gave him the perfect idea for a small business.

"Why not buy a snow plow, attach it to your truck, then clear driveways?" Prefect asked the young acolyte.

"I thought it was a great idea, so I'm gonna buy a snow plow for my Dodge Ram this week and get started." Said Ben.

That sounds good, I guess. A college grad, FAA pilot with instrument ratings, multi-engine, former Marine Captain (like me)...plowing driveways during the Wintertime? All recommended by Prefect.

There's only one problem. What do you do for work in the Spring, Summer, and Fall?

I said my goodbyes and went to bed. I had a very restless night. More nightmares. I was inside a fenced off yard, with a large gothic-type house. Outside was a crowd. Yelling, but I couldn't quite hear them. It seemed they were pleading with me, asking me to escape. But was it me? Or was the crowd calling for their loved ones inside the mansion?

9 BELLY

6am. Time to wakey wakey. Hit the shower, then the road. At the classroom at 7am. A bagel and some pieces of melon, and we're ready to start.

Today we covered more NXIVM principles. Christine told us about how we had a duty to open ethical businesses, because most businesses were unethical. Except for NXIVM businesses of course. We also had some different trainers today. One was Brandon Porter. Brandon was an MD. Yet, he had chosen to give up his emergency room practice and do ESP full-time instead.

To advance in NXIVM and ESP, we had to create businesses – that was the next step. Implement what you have learned. We would each need to start ethical businesses, but first bring the business idea to Prefect or Vanguard for approval. Christine gave us examples of some of the businesses that local ESPians created – a mobile car wash service, a house cleaning service, and a computer repair service. The problem is (and I didn't find this out till later) is that most of these businesses fail.

Most fail, because the operators don't have a real business plan, don't provide services that people use, and their customers are only other ESPians. In fact, the idea behind these businesses is to create a barter service, and thereby decrease your income tax and sales tax exposure. Because if you are not receiving cash, then you don't have to report the transaction and pay taxes on it.

The sinister nature of these businesses came into sharp focus. Their purpose is not to create financial success. But instead, to further insulate ESPians into their ESPian circles. Moreover, if enough ESPians participated, Prefect and Vanguard could create a society within American society. A shadow government, with shadow citizens that lived by their own rules. It's a dark vision of Ayn Rand's teachings.

We could also advance in ESP by recruiting more members. The more members we recruited, the higher our rank. By bringing people in, you would advance more ranks than by just taking classes. In fact, if you recruited someone within 30 days of your first intensive, you would get a permanent mark on your sash, indicating high achievement. I thought about bringing in my younger brother. Surely, he could benefit from ESP.

And there were more classes to take! Many more. Christine said how they had developed around 35 classes. And Vanguard and Prefect were still developing more. Constantly pushing the boundaries and limits of the human intellect. Perfecting the human machine, these classes allowed members to get there – to a place of extreme and authentic human performance. Take the additional classes, and you too could be as smart as Vanguard. But, Christine slipped.

In one of the breaks, she mentioned how she really likes teaching the five-day intensive. She likes it, because she said (and Vanguard had told her) the most important lessons were in the five-day. The basics were the best. Master the basics and you have mastered the course.

Really? Really. So, in other words, did Christine just say the other classes were bullshit? Yessir she did! Oops. There goes the neighborhood. I didn't say anything, I just kept nodding my head and took a mental note. The only important course was the first one. The rest were just fluff. Wow.

So you mean people can spend years taking additional courses, at least 35 and more coming soon, but that the class takers would make no further progress than in the five day basic class? Yep. Hmmm...that sounds strangely similar to Scientology and 'the Bridge'. Take a decade of classes, to learn that none of the additional classes were necessary. Ouch. What a mindfuck!

We also learned about techniques to win arguments and make people like you. If someone was having an argument with you, the normal response is to ask the other person to calm down, re-access the conflict, see what can be done. Not with ESP. For ESPians, the proper response is to get in that person's face and raise your voice also. This throws the provocateur off base. You continue this until the other person backs down.

Mirroring is the way to make people like you. If you want someone to like you, you should mirror their movements. If they are sitting next to you, mirror the way they sit. Copy their pose. If they are sitting, legs crossed – cross your legs also. Look at how they are holding their arms and hands. Do that too. If they take a drink of water, drink water at the same time. Mirror them. By mirroring them, the other person will subconsciously see that as an affirmation of their self-importance. And we all like to believe we are important – don't we?

If you want someone to like you, you should also pretend to be interested in the same topics they are. Someone likes camel racing? Well, claim you are a big fan also. They are interested in growing succulents? Well, like that too.

I also noticed I was really attracted to one of my classmates. She was a really cute, petite blonde. Her boyfriend told her to take the course (he wanted to advance in NXIVM also). Every day she seemed more and more attractive. I was really hot for her. During one of the breaks, I heard some visiting coaches in the atrium (ESPians, but not teaching our course) mention how over time, class members usually start dating and hooking up. They also said how the EMs were a reset for your brain. More side effects of the training.

The day whizzed by. It was 5pm, but it felt like only 10 minutes had passed. We took a quick break, ate some veggies and hummus. I had some tea also and a cookie. And back to it.

The final section that evening was to see an EM. Christine explained that EM stood for 'Exploration of Meaning'. It was a way to heal past traumas, assign new meanings to uncomfortable situations, and to reach a state of bliss. Sounds good right?

Welp, I was going to find out. Christine explained that we needed a volunteer. Right off the bat, she chose me. I was hesitant because multiple cameras were set up when we left the room. So now, I would have to do an EM for the first time. And all of it would be caught on tape. You mean I would have to disclose something very painful? And it would be recorded for Vanguard, Prefect, and all ESPians to see? Pretty much.

I could almost hear the announcer in my mind:

"Step right up, ladies and gentlemen. Welcome to the circus. Here we have the freak of the week (or Weak). You will be amazed by what you see. Stranger than the Fijian mermaid, stronger than He-man, denser than Andre the Giant. Come on in!"

I felt really uncomfortable. Heck with it, just jump in. Cameras were rolling. Action!

I went over a very painful incident from childhood. I was in tears. Looking back now, as a forty-year-old, it seems silly. It was an argument that my mother and father were having. But, I was a kid. It was painful to me. And I had to relive it.

Through a series of questions, Christine brought me right back to the moment. I was in 1984. I was living it. I could taste it. I was there. And I was bawling. The hot tears rolled down my face. Christine took me right to the edge and pulled me back.

With more questions from Christine, I was able to release that anchored memory. Christine used the EM to reprogram me and let go of the pain. Afterwards, it was gone. The painful memory disappeared. The association was gone. It was all gone, like it never happened.

To this day, I could hear or see that emotional trigger, and nothing would happen. It no longer has meaning for me. It doesn't mean anything. It's like it never happened. I can't explain it, other than somehow, someway, NXIVM and ESP has figured out a way to reprogram your brain. It truly is an amazing technology – the EM. I wish I had done more. I sure could use them.

Wouldn't it be great, if you could erase all of your bad memories and live in bliss? Hells to the yeah! Sign me up buttercup. But, it is worth it, if the cost is your *soul?*

Your identity forever gone? Is that a fair price? Because we are a collection of our emotional experiences – our successes, failures, and tragedies. If you have compassion for someone, it is likely because you experienced the same hardship or trauma. But, if you erased the trauma...would you still have the same level of compassion? Would you recognize the new 'you'?

That night, I had a call from my Executive Producer of Heaven in Exile – my good friend Aaron Bleich. I've known Aaron more than 20 years. One of the nicest people you will ever meet. And a talented producer – the guy won an Emmy for his news coverage during 9/11.

He was calling because he loved the demo reel and the movie. He was ecstatic!

"Great job! I'm proud of you. You really nailed it!" He said.

"Okay. Sounds good." I replied. Then silence.

"What do you mean? Are you okay?" Asked Aaron.

"Yes, doing fine. Everything okay." I said, almost in a monotone.

"Buddy, you sound dead. Why aren't you excited?" He asked.

"Not really sure. Just trying to manage my emotional state." I answered.

The NXIVM training was really starting to kick in. In ESP we are taught to seek an emotional baseline – don't get too excited, don't get too sad. Stay level headed. You can experience major emotions during EMs, but not during normal hours.

And feelings. The side effect of the EMs is that they attack your brain's emotional center. By reducing the emotional intensity of memories, *all* of your emotions are reduced. In a sense, Aaron was right. I was dying.

That night, I kept having another nightmare. As snow fell on the neighborhood and covered everything in a puffy white blanket, a person was walking around. He would walk to a house, look in the window, then walk to the next house. But he was walking on the roofs also!

To get to the next house, he would walk up the side of the house, up the roof, and down the other side. And the footprints were odd. They were steaming! Little wisps of steam were rising from where the creature had stepped.

As I walked closer to take a look, I noticed something else. Instead of a normal footprint, the stranger was leaving hoof marks! Strange dreams indeed.

10 REVEAL

Up at 6am, quick shower. Hit the road. And back to class, ready to start.

Thursday was kind of a blur. The day went by fast. I remember seeing the cute blonde again. We spoke more during one of the breaks. I could tell the feelings were mutual. As we talked, she began to blush and look downwards while smiling. Definitely a good sign.

In class, we talked about using EMs to anchor and revisit positive memories. To do this, we would each break off with a coach who would do an EM with us. Even our normal coaches, Ariella and Javier, would get EMs done by other ESPians. They were excited!

During the last part of the day, each of us underwent an Experience of Meaning to anchor or modify an emotion. My coach for the EM was an attractive brunette lady, late 30s, that had stopped in to help with the EMs. She asked if I there was a certain painful experience I wanted to revisit.

"No thanks!!!" I responded. I just finished reliving the painful childhood one, the night before. Let's do a fun one. The neat part about the EMs is that they can anchor positive emotions as well. We sat down and we started.

"Tell me about a really positive experience in your life." Asked the coach.

"Well, meeting the Dalai Lama was a highlight." I answered.

"What do you remember, right before you met him?" Asked the dark-haired beauty.

"I remember setting up the cameras, positioning the seats, getting ready for the interview." I said.

"How did that make you feel?" She asked.

"Really good." I said.

"Why did that make you feel good?" She continued.

"Well, because it was the completion of a goal. Working for months to get an interview. Traveling to India, managing the crew. Meeting everyone. It was a ton of work." I answered.

"And how did you feel?" The attractive coach asked.

"I felt great. I felt so happy." I noted.

"Okay, and how did you feel when you saw him?" She asked.

"Even more happy." I replied.

Now she began to challenge and change my anchor point.

"Okay, so how did the Dalai Lama feel?" She asked.

"I don't know." I answered.

"You really can't tell what his inner feelings were, can you?" She continued.

"Nope, you can't." I said.

"So really, the feeling is all within you." She answered.

"Ohhhhhhhh..." I said.

The purpose of the positive EM is to re-experience a highlight of your life. Then through a series of questions, the coach teaches you that the highlights (and the positive emotions) are only in your mind. That is, there are no outside forces that gave you this feeling. You came up with these feelings all by yourself. You created your mental state, and your reality. And therefore, you can revisit this positive emotion anytime. Because it's all in your mind.

It's really not that complicated. If anything, it is a modification of a Tony Robbins technique called anchoring and backwards view. If you can anchor a positive emotional state, you can feel that emotion anytime you want to. Conversely, if you want to get rid of a negative emotional state, play the mental picture of the episode backwards in your mind. Make the aggressors cartoonish. Make them look like mice, or dweebs, or gnomes. Put them in underwear! Purple polka dot underwear. Change their voices. You get the idea.

By changing the experience, you can change the anchor point, and your destiny. It's a rehash of Tony Robbins. That's all the Exploration of Meaning (or EM) is. It is merely a Tony Robbins exercise packaged in some technobabble. Not original or made by NXIVM at all.

The classes finished late that evening. On my way out of the atrium, I was approached by Brandon – the doctor. He asked how the classes were going. I said really good. The EMs are amazing. He agreed.

He then asked if I wanted to play volleyball and meet Vanguard that night.

Sure! I responded. Why not...

Brandon came over at about 10pm. We talked to Ben for awhile. Then we hit the road. We arrived at Hayner Sports Barn in Halfmoon, NY. The township is about 20 miles from Albany. In New England, all of the villages and small townships are minutes away from each other. Different from Texas. Back home, multiple highways run through the state, and you can spend hours driving and never see a town.

The Hayner Sports Barn is like a big gym complex. It has multiple basketball rims and backboards (that can be raised and lowered), retractable wooden gym seats, and volleyball nets. Inside, a group was sitting down on the gym seats. One ESPian was giving an EM to another ESPian. I recognized the 'recipient' of the EM – actress Nicki Clyne from the Battlestar Galactica reboot. The coach and Nicki were chatting away.

Another group was standing. And further away, a larger group was sitting. And in the center of the larger group, was Keith Raniere – the Vanguard. Would he remember me? Can he watch me play volleyball and reveal the secrets of my personality? It all seemed possible. He was the Vanguard of course!

I noticed other people around Vanguard. One was a very slender dark-haired woman. Clare! Another was a younger looking and more bubbly strawberry blonde. Sara! This is Clare and Sara Bronfman. The Seagram heiresses. I remembered seeing them on stage with the Dalai Lama in Albany. Clare???

Clare has a slight British accent. She speaks good English, very slow and measured. But I was shocked by her appearance. Her hair was pulled back into a pony tail. Her features were austere. No makeup, rail thin, her skin looked a tint of green. She looked sickly.

Clare looked like she stepped out of 1865, or maybe Little House on the Prairie. Schoolmarm city! Sara was a bit shy and awkward. We spoke for a few minutes about world travel. The heiresses had been to many places, but not Bhutan. I told them about the Dragon Country, the land of the Shabdrung and Guru Rinpoche, and Buddhist ghosts that I wrote about in *Elemental Shaman*. I also told them I could get a triple-engine helicopter, if they needed one. That is definitely the way to travel in Bhutan.

But still...Clare! I found out later she was younger than Sara and younger than me. At the time, she was 31. But she looked 45! About that time, Vanguard got up and walked to the volleyball net. He was ready to play.

Keith Raniere has a very distinct walk. He walks on the balls of his feet, kind of rolls them. As he walks, he shifts side to side. It's almost like a waddle. Like a monkey walk actually, because he leads with the top of his torso. You will never forget it, if you see it.

They played a few rounds, then asked me to join. I was going to stand next to Vanguard (so he could see my moves and tell me the secrets of my soul). But Clare stopped me very quickly.

"Omar." Said the heiress. "Move right there." As she said this, she pointed to a spot to her left and behind Big V.

"Sure," I responded. And we played a few rounds of volleyball. Not even a full game. I didn't even get to serve. And Keith never told me the secrets to my soul.

Afterwards, Keith walked to and sat on the rolled-up gym mat across from the volleyball court. I drifted to Vanguard.

"Vanguard! Good to see you again." I said.

"Hey, how are you?" He answered.

"I'm well thanks." I replied. "You remember me, we met at ..." my voice trailed. I wanted to see if he remembered me from the Dalai Lama teaching in Albany, where he was dressed black on black, wavy hair, short grey beard – guru style.

"Ummm...ummm. Lemme think. Ummm..." He said.

I let him squirm for about 30 seconds. Obviously, he couldn't remember me. Thus far, the score was Truth 2, Vanguard 0. Keith didn't seem to have any supernatural or paranormal powers. He couldn't tell my personality from playing volleyball. And he sure as hell didn't remember my name.

Okay, let's try some more. Time to test the saucier...

"So what do you think of psychic phenomena as an after-effect of deep meditation?" I asked.

The Vanguard replied, "Well, the Buddhists in the Kala Sutra tell us that meditation, or no mind, is the ultimate goal and one should not be obsessed or pulled by psychic experiences."

Welp, that's true. I did read that before. But there is no book named the Kala Sutra. Kamalashila was a Buddhist master. The Kama Sutra is well, the Kama Sutra. But there is no Kala Sutra...

"And what about UFOs, do you think they are real?" I asked.

"I've seen some stuff. I think they exist. But obviously, they are more powerful than us and mean us no harm" He replied.

"So, if they really wanted to harm us, we wouldn't be having this conversation." I finished.

"That's right." He answered.

And that was it. There was no great awakening, no great knowledge. He wasn't a brainiac, but he wasn't the devil either. Just a guy with some knowledge. Not every impressive.

I realize now that Vanguard was just mirroring me. By pretending to be interested in my questions, he hoped to establish a bond and get me to like him. By rephrasing my questions and spinning them back at me, he wanted me to believe he was super intelligent. Well, he wasn't. To this day, he's just Keith. At least to me.

I thanked Big Vanguard and walked away. I was heading to our van and Brandon was giving me a ride back to Ginger's house. On the drive back, I thought about the peaceful scenery of the rolling hills, covered in fluffy white snow. A thick blanket of snow gives everything a divine stillness. At nighttime, snow deadens sound. With a starry night, a thick layer of snow can seem almost celestial as the evening world becomes cotton and stars.

As we drove back, I thought about all I had learned. What EMs were, was ESP about, how to advance in NXIVM. There was something strange though.

During the volleyball game with Vanguard, one of his followers was leaving early. She was an attractive Latina lady, about 25, thin, good-looking, long dark hair. Vanguard stopped the game and called her over to him, before she left.

"Hey Christina." He said. "Don't forget to kiss me before you leave."

As she approached Keith, he raised his lips and then gave her a full tongue kiss. Every woman was required to say goodbye and hello to Vanguard like this. At least the thin, attractive, young women.

That's kinda weird. I don't usually say hello to women like that. Or order them to kiss me, before they leave a room.

11 RISE

On Friday we finished our last class. Quickly, we recapped the most important parts. NXIVM was an ethical foundation. The ethos of ESP was to obtain as many of the world's resources as possible and use them in an ethical way. Our next step was to start ethical businesses (Nancy and Vanguard-approved of course). And never, ever reveal the secrets of NXIVM or use the word 'cult'.

I felt very positive about the program. We learned to adjust our focus with EMs. We were giving a new heading, a new life and direction. And everyone that fought us in the outside world were parasites. Because they took and stole our energy. Best way to deal with parasites: cut them from your life.

Christine presented us with sashes. I still have mine. White with one flash. And we also learned the secret handshake. (It was actually a hand grasp). We would use this to quickly and secretly identify other ESPians in the world. And if you recruited another member within 30 days, you would get a special color flash on your sash that you could wear forever.

The cute blonde was leaving. She was headed to New York for the weekend. I wish I had tagged along. But, I needed to get back to Vancouver to finish up editing of my film.

Tabby picked me up and took me to the airport. As she was dropping me off, she asked me if I could spare any gas money. Of course. I felt really bad – I gave her $20. She had moved to Albany to do NXIVM full-time. But, her website business was failing. Working on self-improvement with ESP had cost her time and money.

We said our goodbyes. I thanked Tabby again for the classes. As I was walking through the airport, I noticed something. I didn't see other people anymore. Instead, I saw blue luminous globes of light. Each light was a consciousness. I was actually seeing people as manifestations of the universe - a universe conscious of itself. Each person was generating consciousness. It was amazing!

I could also see my own thoughts and go into deeper levels of meditation. Seeing your own thoughts is akin to stepping out of your thought process. It feels like an out-of-body experience, but you are totally awake. It's an enlightening meditation. It's sort of like being awake, but watching yourself on a TV screen. I could quickly *see* and register my thoughts about happiness, my fears, and my dreams. If you can see your thoughts, you can easily modify them and not be beholden to them. I could change the associations that my thoughts created instantly, without the EMs.

Why do we get nervous about public speaking? Why do I become shy around attractive women? Why do I like popcorn? These are all thoughts based on patterns. Recognize the pattern, quickly alter it, and change the thought forever. It's pretty amazing stuff.

And beyond that, the mediation allows you to feel things in a different way. It feels like thinking with another part of your brain. If during normal consciousness, your mind is slightly in front of your eyes – this instead feels like your mind is tucked behind your head. This meditative state allows you to sense things in a different way.

The ordinary becomes extraordinary. The mundane, divine. Virtually anything you do, becomes an activity in bliss. You could make an experience out of lifting up a pencil. Drinking a simple glass of water can bring you an emotional high. And it gives you a runner's high, but without the sweat. I've tried it before, but my brother said I was starting to look spaced-out. Almost glazed.

As my plane lifted off, and headed back home, I was lost in thought. What would this brave new world be like? How many new adventures could be lived? How many different people could I be?

Yet, there was something bothering me from earlier. As I was leaving the classroom for the last time, Christine pulled me aside.

"How did you like the classes?" She asked.

"Really awesome. Everything was great." I said.

"Was there anything you had problems with?" Christine asked.

"Not really. I thought the whole bowing to the room thing and saying 'Thank you Vanguard' was kinda silly." I noted.

"Well, that's just you not fully integrating the training. You need to get past those blocks to really learn from the program." She noted. "And I really think you didn't grasp the concepts. Maybe you should take more classes."

Huh? What do you mean? I did understand it. It was a great program. I learned about EMs, deep meditation, and observing my own thoughts and patterns.

I learned later on, this happens *every* time. At the end of the course, the proctor will take the top students aside, and suggest they take *more* classes. By challenging the student's grasp of the training, the student feels compelled to take more classes to prove themselves. There are 35 more courses to choose from. And there were more classes being created by Vanguard and Prefect.

Pretty slick, huh? Pretty slick indeed. What a mindfuck.

12 FALLEN

I was back in Vancouver on Thursday, December 17. It was the week before Christmas. I was working on the footage from Heaven in Exile, trying to get that last bit of polish.

I looked at Facebook to see if any local NXIVM and ESP groups were around. Sure enough, there was a chapter in Vancouver. When you complete your ESP training, you are taught that other ESPians are your friends. You are part of a society, created to improve the world and bring the planet into an ethical age.

There's even a secret handshake. Ask me, I will show you. And there's even a double-secret handshake, meant only for those who recruited others within 30 days of getting a new colored sash. We all received white sashes with one stripe, and I have mine...somewhere.

And on Facebook, there was going to be an ESP meet-up at a local bar on Saturday evening. New recruits were going to be told about the program. And Nancy Salzman was going to be there! Prefect in the flesh. I was stoked. Chance to meet other ESPians and Nancy. Sounds good right?

Saturday evening came, I drove to the restaurant bar and walked up the stairs to the venue. I recognized a few faces. During the week, I had made Facebook friends with some of these people. I introduced myself, walked around, spread the Kool-Aid to the prospects.

You see, the Vanguard was a cool dude. The ESP program was great and not a cult at all. No way. I told the same thing to about 4 people – I was hesitant at first, but after taking the class, I really liked it.

I also found out the Vancouver ESPians were taking a trip to Whistler Ski Resort (about a two-hour drive north of Vancouver) over Christmas. So instead of spending time with their blood relatives for Boxing Day, the ESPians would be bonding on the ski slopes. Weird!

About the same time, the tall man in Khaki showed up. The one from Albany. Mark Vicente.

Mark was organizing the band, directing them where to setup their equipment. I tried to introduce myself.

"Hey Mark. How's it going?" I asked.

"Not now. I'm busy." He gruffly replied.

"I just wanted to introduce myself. I'm Omar from the Albany group." I said.

"NOT NOW, DIDN'T YOU HEAR WHAT I JUST SAID!" He yelled at me.

Okay dude. Sorry to bother your rocket surgery. I walked back to the others. After a few moments, I ordered a drink and some food. Drinks were on Mark Hildreth. He was a local Vancouver actor and NXIVM student. High ranking. And drinks were on him. Sounds good.

So, I ordered a drink and food. Sat down. About 3 minutes later, there was a commotion. A bunch of cellphones went off. One, then another, then another. All in series. In all, like 5 phones must have gone off.

Did someone die? Was Nancy Salzman okay? I was looking forward to meeting her and asking more about how she started NXIVM and why she decided to use Tony Robbins techniques.

As soon as the people answered their phones, they began to ask... "Where's Omar?" and "Who's Omar?"

Well, that's me. Sitting down. Just sipping on a drink and ordered some food. They looked around after a few minutes and spotted me.

"Are you Omar?" they asked. Welp, yeah. "Stay right there," they said.

Within about 30 seconds, Mark Vicente and 3 other guys surrounded me. Mark was the 'ringleader' and the blonde guy with him was Lucas Roberts (Roberts now runs a failing computer repair shop in Vancouver. The shop is failing because he spent all his money and time on NXIVM courses). They brought along two armed goons. I could tell the bodyguards were armed, because there was a bulge under their sports coats. Right where I would put a gun in a holster, if I was armed.

That's strange. How do you get handguns in Canada? I thought that was illegal.

Mark sat right next to me and began questioning me. His tone was hostile.

"What are you doing here?" He asked.

I answered, "I took the ESP classes in Albany. I'm back in Vancouver and wanted to meet Prefect."

"Well, how did you find out about this place?" He continued.

"It was on Facebook, an event for ESP members in Vancouver," I answered.

"How did you know it was here?" Mark demanded.

"It was on the flyer. Party at 8pm, Prefect was attending." I told him.

Mark finally revealed what the issue was. He kept glaring at me, challenging me.

"Well, we heard you were working on a film." Said the Enforcer.

"Yep. It's almost finished." I responded. Then a series of 5 questions from Mark and the blonde guy.

"What's it about?"
"Where did you film it?"
"When is it being released?"
"Who is your producer?"
"Where was it filmed?"
"What's it about?"

About that time, they started to repeat their questions. Obviously, my answer is not going to change if you ask me the same thing 10 times. You can put a firearm to my head. My answer is not going to be different. That is just my personality. If anything, I start to get sarcastic.

Mark told me how they didn't know what my film was about, and if my film was going to be about NXIVM. Because, he was the exclusive filmmaker for the group. Mark Vicente then told me how Kristin Kreuk was a very senior member of NXIVM, a top member that was the face of group. He also said that she didn't like to be bothered by directors or filmmakers.

I really didn't understand what he was talking about. I was there to meet Prefect. Not an actress that just bombed with her role in Street Fighter: The Legend of Chun Li. As Mark was talking and sitting next to me, I began to use the body mirroring techniques that Christine and NXIVM taught me. As Mark crossed his legs, I crossed my legs. As he held his hand under his head, I did the same thing.

Mimicry was supposed to make someone like you and calm them down. Well, it didn't work. Instead, Mark went full on Pulp Fiction...

"Well, you know I just completed a film too." He said. "Are you editing, is your sound locked?" Mark Vicente asked.

Well fuck, obviously if I'm still editing, the sound isn't locked. Hello dumbass. This was the great director? The Great Mark Vicente? Seriously? He didn't seem so great to me. Just another ESPian who was exaggerating their credentials.

"In my film, I spent weeks with dangerous Cartel members in Mexico. Really evil guys. I visited them in Mexico City, in jails, and in prisons. That's what *my* film is about." Mark said as he emphasized the *my* part.

"And you know, these are ordinary looking guys. Really normal. But, they've done the most horrible things." Mark continued. "In fact, you could be sitting right next to one, and never even know it." He said. "A person is never safe. In Canada or the USA."

Ahhhh...I gotcha. What he was trying to say (what Mark Vicente was telling me) is that he had Cartel connections. That is why he had access to cartel members in Mexican jails. And he could reach out, and touch me with his connections, anytime he wanted to. That's very dark. I was not expecting that. I didn't know what to say.

It is not a normal thing to say – I know people in the Cartel that can harm you anytime, anywhere. Why would Mark say that?

"Okay then. I'm going to go ahead and get going." I said.

Mark replied, "That's a good idea. We'll walk you out."

I didn't have any weapons. Two of Mark's three goons were carrying guns. It was a closed area, nowhere to really run or hide if gunshots start going off. Did I really want to get shot tonight? It wasn't on my list of things to-do.

Mark Vicente walked me down the stairs and led me out the front door. The goons were behind me. Armed. Not smart for me, but I didn't have a choice. As I walked out the building and looked back, I saw Mark place one of the goons outside the entrance. The muscle adjusted his pants, reached to his right and secured something on his side. With the reflection of the streetlights, I saw a flash of silver metal.

It was a pistol. Looked like a .45. And with that, I was done.

I was never invited to any other NXIVM events, never asked to take any other classes, never asked to hit V-Week (Vanguard's 10-day long birthday celebration. An observant blogger noted, not even Kim Jong-Un has 10-day long birthday celebrations).

All because of a film I was working on...about Tibetan refugees?

But everything worked out in the end. Maybe it was fate. Maybe it was just dumb luck smiling on me that day. Because I would have taken more classes. Of course, I would have taken more classes! The classes were great. Everyone was awesome. Or so I thought.

Ten years later, the truth came out...

13 SUNLIGHT

On October 21, 2017, the story broke in the New York Times. At first, I didn't believe it:

INSIDE A SECRETIVE GROUP WHERE WOMEN ARE BRANDED

ALBANY – Last March, five women gathered in a home near here to enter a secret sisterhood...

The story continued, describing the initiation into DOS, which seemed more like torture.
The new recruits were told they were going to become members of a female empowerment group. Instead, they were kidnapped, raped, and mutilated. You see, DOS stands for Dominus Obsequious Sororium...which really means 'Master over Slave Women'.

The women were blindfolded, taken to a room, and

forced to hold one another down as Dr. Danielle Roberts burned initials near their vaginas. Not branded, but seared into the flesh with multiple passes of a surgical cauterizing pen. The initials KR and AM stood for the group's leaders – Keith Raniere and Allison Mack. Raniere is also known in some circles by his cult leader name – Vanguard.

What the holy hell? Did I just read that? Allie Mack? And Keith? They're now sex slavers? And they kidnapped women and burned the initials KR and AM near the victims' vaginas? Nah, it can't be possible. What is this, Weekly World News? Is this a joke?

For a couple of days, I didn't believe the story. And I kept making excuses for Keith. Ahhh...it was just a little brand. C'mon now, these are grown adults – this is probably a sex game gone haywire. Allie is an actress, supposed to be all about female empowerment. Why would she ever place her brand on another woman? Are women cattle to Allie Mack? Couldn't be true. No way, no how.

I even contacted Dr. Brandon Porter via Facebook IM. I gave him words of support. I knew Sarah Edmonson. And I had a run-in with Mark Vicente. They must be lying. The story can't be true. Brandon thanked me for the support. He was very tight-lipped though. He didn't reveal anything other than 'We're aware, it sucks'. And I wasn't going to press. He was my friend, after all. He was family. You see, 10 years later, the bonds of the Cult still run strong.

It took me a week to process everything. As the days passed, the illusion was finally broken. More and more reports emerged of the torture, the ghastly abuse, the sheer abomination of this group. Have you ever smelled human flesh burn? I have. You never forget that smell. It smells like a sickly, sweet pork chop. Never forget that smell. Till the day I die, I will always remember.

How could anyone possibly do that to another human being? Burn them multiple times, to mark them with another person's initials. It wasn't a hot iron or brand – painful for a few seconds, then done. This was a burning of living skin, layer by later. Reports said the mark on each victim took 20 minutes to make. And it was done without anesthesia. Without anesthetics?!?! Yes, without any type of anesthetic. My dear God. What are these animals doing?

As more and more information came out, the crystal castle was completely shattered. I think the escape points for me were seeing Allie Mack in Mexico, emaciated, chasing down Federal Police after they captured her master, the Vanguard Keith Raniere. Allie looked like she stepped out of a POW camp. She looked like a walking skeleton. The group was staying in a $10,000 a week mansion in Puerto Vallarta. Plenty of food to eat, plenty of money. Yet, the skeleton that was Allison Mack looked starved and incoherent. How do you go from a hit TV show, and being an attractive blonde, to looking like an extra from the Walking Dead? But for real?

The other breaking point was seeing Vanguard's GPA. You see, for years Prefect Nancy Salzman and

Vanguard Keith had bragged that Keith was one of the smartest people on the planet. Started talking in complete sentences by age 2. State Judo champion at age 12. Tied the State 100-yard dash record while in High School. Graduated with multiple degrees from Rensselaer Polytechnic. Now, let's stop right there.

Because the FBI actually pulled Vanguard's GPA from Rensselaer (pronounced rens-suh-LEER). And you know what it was? 2.26! Yes, that's right – a fucking 2.26. From the World's Smartest Man? And Rensselaer isn't even a top ten school. It isn't even a top 40 school. Hell, my GPA was higher than VanGrifters!

And Keith Raniere is just that – a liar, a crook, and a conman. We all got conned. None of it was real. The accolades, the intelligence, the focus, the not having to sleep but 2 hours a day, the veganism (I found out later that Keith loves Cheeseburgers. Heck, don't we all?).

And the MEGA Test? The test that established Keith as one of the highest IQs on the planet. One of the smartest people that ever walked the Earth. What about that one?

Welp, it turns out, the MEGA Test is a fake test too. None of the diagnostic groups (American Psychiatric Association, American Psychological Association) recognize the MEGA Test because it is: 1) a take-home exam and 2) has no time limit. Well, what the hell kind of test is that, if it's a take-home test, and it's not timed? Obviously, someone could get a copy, then hire a team of college students and teachers to take the exam for them. And that is exactly what VanGrifter did.

Heck, we could make our own IQ Test. Call it the ULTRA MIND IQ. Sounds pretty fancy, huh? Well guess who scores it? Me. And guess who writes the questions? Me. And guess who obtained the world's #3 score and is one of the smartest people on the planet? You guessed it... ME! It's a joke, but it's not funny. Because that is exactly what Keith Raniere did.

And that is how these senior Cult members operate. I saw the same thing with Nancy. I saw the same thing with other senior Cult members listed in the dossier portion of this book. They give themselves fancy titles and certifications that no one can verify. Then, they self-promote as experts, successful business people, leaders in the field of human development psychobabble. But, it's all a sham. None of it is real. It's a fugazzi.

And the first intensive, the five-day, is a great program. It can really help you think in unique ways, reset your brain, and get you to deeper levels of meditation. But after that, the other classes are just rehash. They are illusory. They are superfluous bullshit. Like putting extra layers of chocolate icing, on a chocolate cake. Well, it's good for the first layer. But after that, you're just adding frosting. And it doesn't make the cake better – it makes it worse.

And the class is not some mind-blowing science. All Nancy and Keith did was rehash Tony Robbins, Scientology, and thrown in some Ayn Rand for good measure. Mix it all up, and you get ESP. Yet, Prefect and Vanguard never really describe what the Executive Success Program is. Instead, they give you a word salad. A non-stop list of words that don't mean anything.

For instance, if you asked me, why do we have global warming? A simple answer would be, "Well, scientists differ. Most scientists agree that global warming is due to increased levels of carbon dioxide in the atmosphere due to manmade pollution." Fair enough.

Vanguard would say, "Global warming is a concerning phenomenon, due to an individual's quest for existential meaning on the planet. It is on this quest, that one can find true authenticity as they search for self. This is the authentic journey."

Okay, so what the fuck does that mean? It doesn't mean anything. Vanguard is just rephrasing your question and spinning it back at you.

Keith is validating your question, by basically saying 'good question'. By giving validity to your question, you automatically like Vanguard and now think he is smart because he just gave you some approval. In other words, it's a rehash. Remember that part of the class, when I told you that Christine taught us to 'mirror' a person so that they would like us? This is the same thing, but with words. Vanguard is just mirroring your question and spitting it back at you, so that you feel you've obtained his approval. And we all love approval.

That is the great reveal. The entire ESP course is nonsense. It is a validation for peoples' insecurities. And the groundbreaking 'technology'? There's nothing groundbreaking about it. It's a just a rehash of others' work. And Vanguard's supposed intelligence, is just that – a supposition based on nonsense. Like his nonsense answers. None of it real folks.

That's it. Show's over. Time to go home. But not quite.

Everything worked out well for me. My film was a success, I won a few awards. I got back into my law practice, helping disabled folks. And these clowns were arrested. Or I should say, they are being arrested as I write this.

So now, I present to you the great Dossier. Based on FBI reports, anonymous sources, and personal experience. Now you get to decide who these people are. Are they unfairly accused intellectuals, being targeted by a totalitarian government? Or are they the shadows themselves? Only existing as dark shades and stains, preying on the weakest human beings?

You decide. Let's take a look...

DOSSIER

The information presented in this section is taken from FBI Reports, witness interviews, first-hand accounts, and confidential sources.

KEITH ALLAN RANIERE
Alias: VANGUARD

Sex: Male
Race: White
DOB: 8/26/1960
POB: Brooklyn, NY, USA
Height: 5' 5"
Weight: 185
Eyes: Hazel
Hair: Grey
BOP Number: 57005-177

Alleged Crimes: Sex Trafficking, Conspiracy, Racketeering, Money Laundering, Bulk Cash Smuggling, Tax Evasion, Obstruction

Background Info: Not much is known about Raniere's early background. He was born in Brooklyn, but grew up in Suffern, New York. He attended Rensselaer Polytechnic University and graduated with a 2.26 GPA.

Raniere first came to the attention of law enforcement when he operated a business called Consumers Buyline. The company greatly exaggerated its profits, claiming to have achieved $1 Billion in sales within two years. Consumers Buyline was sued by multiple States Attorneys General and shut down in 1994. The company was deemed to be illegally operating as an MLM (Multi-Level Marketing) Pyramid scheme, where new members' subscription fees were used to pay off old members. The new members would then recruit newer members, who paid additional fees and kept the pyramid scheme going.

Raniere, along with co-founder Nancy Salzman, launched NXIVM in 1998. From the beginning, the suspect lied about and exaggerated his accomplishments including:

Programming computers in 1973 (when modern programming languages did not exist);
State Judo Champion at age 12 (No one can verify);
100-yard Dash Champion in High School (Debunked, because in 1970s, event was 100-meter sprint, not 100-yard dash);

World's Top 3 Smartest People (Debunked, MEGA Test is a take-home exam, with no time limits, and not recognized by any Psychological Testing Association); Sleeps two hours a night (Debunked, Raniere actually sleeps all day according to multiple witnesses); Invented video teleconferencing (Debunked, Patent is owned by AT&T and Microsoft)

Alleged Criminal Activity: As head of the NXIVM crime organization, Raniere is responsible for the management, supervision, and operation of the enterprise. Many have described Raniere's organization as 'Cult-like' or a 'Cult' due to Raniere's insistence on worship, praise, a hierarchical structure, and that followers call him 'Vanguard' or leader.

However, this is not illegal. It is the associated activities from the operation of NXIVM that constitute alleged criminal activity.

Sex Trafficking: Raniere is accused of creating a sub-unit of NXIVM that operated as a sexual slavery ring. With help from Co-Conspirator 1 (later identified by the FBI as Allison Mack), Raniere designed a pyramid scheme of forced labor where he gave himself the rank of Grandmaster. The Grandmaster would then have six Slave Masters underneath him. Each Slave Master was to operate a slave pod with six slaves. The slaves were subjected to low-calorie diets, sleep deprivation, forced labor without monetary compensation, branding, and sexual acts. The slaves were also told that if they complained to authorities: 1) compromising information including slaves' nude photographs would be released, 2) slaves' property would be sold and transferred to Raniere, and 3) damaging criminal evidence about each slave would be divulged.

Raniere's involvement has been corroborated by signals intelligence, witness statements, text messages, and wiretaps. After the arrest warrant was issued, Raniere was captured in Puerto Vallarta, Mexico while staying in a $10,000 a week luxury villa. After apprehension, the Mexican Federal Police vehicle transporting Raniere was chased at high speeds by NXIVM members Allison Mack and Nicki Clyne. The situation almost led to a shootout.

Raniere's involvement in the day-to-day operation of NXIVM is somewhat unknown. During the course of

NXIVM operations, the organization allegedly engaged in bulk cash smuggling from Mexico to Albany, NY, using private jets as means of transport.

It is also believed that Raniere never declared the millions of dollars in cash gifts from the Bronfman sisters as taxable income. In addition, although Raniere claims to receive no personal income and be a pauper, at the time of his arrest he was using a checking account with a balance of over $8 Million USD. It also believed that on Raniere's orders, attorneys and judicial officials in Mexico were bribed to issue arrest warrants against witnesses who have cooperated with the FBI.

WARNING: Approach with caution. Raniere has legions of devoted followers, exhibits traits of psychopathy, and can hypnotize people through long conversations and use of word loops or mental suggestion.

NANCY L. SALZMAN
Alias: PREFECT, DON NANCY, THE GODMOTHER

Sex: Female
Race: White
DOB: 1954
POB: Unknown
Height: 5' 6"
Weight: 155
Eyes: Brown
Hair: Brown
BOP Number: None yet Assigned

Alleged Crimes: Racketeering, Money Laundering, Bulk Cash Smuggling, Tax Evasion

Background Info: Not much is known about Salzman's early background. She is a registered nurse in the state of

New York, under license 362518. Her residence is listed as Waterford, New York. Since the arrest of Keith Raniere by the FBI, Salzman has not been seen.

Salzman was working as a pediatric nurse when she met Keith Raniere in the mid-90s. Together the two started NXIVM and ESP (Executive Success Programs). The umbrella organization NXIVM was described as teaching self-improvement courses and leadership principles. However, the most beneficial course was the 5-day intensive. After the first courses, the additional 35 courses had no benefit, other than taking money from students. Students were also encouraged to recruit more members, to obtain financial rewards and rank. This recruiting strategy bears all the hallmarks of an MLM pyramid scheme. As part of his previous settlement with States Attorney Generals, Raniere had agreed to never operate an MLM scheme again.

Racketeering: Salzman is responsible for the day-to-day financial operations of NXIVM and ESP. It is alleged that she managed the books and directed various financial schemes to take money from the Seagram heiresses Clare and Sara Bronfman including commodities speculation, real estate deals in California, and building of office spaces in Albany, New York.

If Salzman obtained illicit funds and re-characterized these funds as legitimate financial gains or business profits, this would be money laundering. It is also alleged by the FBI that Salzman engaged in bulk cash smuggling from Mexico, via transport of cash from NXIVM classes given in Mexico, to Albany, NY. The cash was allegedly transported via private jets owned by the heiresses.

It is also alleged that Salzman failed to completely report her income during the operation of NXIVM and did not pay full taxes on said income. When the FBI agents raided her home at 3 Oregon Trail, Waterford, NY 12188, the agents discovered more than $500,000 USD in cash hidden in shoe boxes, old purses, and drawers. The agents also recovered multiple hard drives, computers, zip drives, burner phones, cameras, and other equipment.

WARNING: Approach with caution. Salzman is believed to be in hiding. She is also a certified hypnotherapist. She may be traveling with large amounts of cash and it is unknown what she might do to defend her money.

ALLISON CHRISTIN MACK
Alias: ALLIE MACK, PIMP MACK

Sex: Female
Race: White
DOB: 7/29/1982
POB: Preetz, West Germany
Height: 5' 5"
Weight: 90
Eyes: Blue
Hair: Brown (natural) or Blonde
BOP Number: 90838-053

Alleged Crimes: Sex Trafficking, Sex Trafficking Conspiracy, Forced Labor Conspiracy, Immigration Fraud

Background Info: Mack grew up in Los Angeles and was exposed to acting at a young age. Her break came in the hit CW TV series Smallville. Mack played Clark Kent's sidekick Chloe Sullivan. Fans remember her character having a 'Wall of Weird' where the plucky reporter would track supernatural or strange events in Smallville.

Mack started NXIVM in 2008 and was recruited by Kristin Kreuk. At first, Mack's involvement in NXIVM and ESP was minimal, but she was groomed by Keith Raniere and Nancy Salzman for senior leadership positions.

In 2017, it was revealed that Mack and Raniere established a sub-group of NXIVM called DOS for Dominus Obsequious Sororium (Master over Slave Women or Dominant Over Submissive). The group operated on a pyramid scheme structure, with Keith Raniere at the top of the pyramid as 'Grandmaster'. Mack was told to recruit slaves, which then would then make her a Master. The slaves would then recruit other slaves and the pods would function in groups of 6. The Grand Master would have 6 slaves, where the slaves would then have 6 slaves each, and those slaves would have 6 slaves for a pod structure of 666.

The women slaves were lured in with the promise of joining a 'Badass Bitch Bootcamp' and female empowerment group. Instead, the slaves were subjected to starvation diets, sleep depravation, and unwanted sexual activities. To keep the slaves under bondage, the slaves were made to submit sexually graphic photographs, confessions of past criminal activity, and deeds to homes, real estate, and unborn children. If the slaves broke ranks or told anyone about DOS, the blackmail material would be released.

At the same time Mack was an alleged SlaveMaster in DOS, she contacted famous Hollywood actresses to ask them to join a 'female empowerment group'. The people Mack contacted via Twitter included Emma Watson, Kelly Clarkson, and Samia Shoab. Mack also attempted to recruit authors Amanda Hess, Jill Filipovic, and Jennifer Pastiloff.

Slaves were burned with initials of Keith Raniere and Allison Mack – KR and AM near their pubic region, with a cauterizing iron. The marks were created by the iron being passed over the skin multiple times, with no anesthetics being used. The slaves were then told to wrap the damaged tissue with plastic, to increase scarification and delay healing. The procedure was performed by Dr.

Danielle Roberts, D.O. of Clifton Park, NY, Medical License 255075.

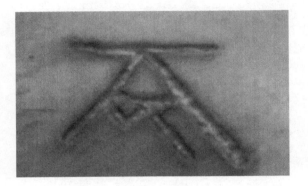

It is also alleged that Mack married Canadian actress Nicki Clyne, so that Clyne could remain in the United States and stay within the NXIVM group. However, the marriage is questionable, as NXIVM encourages such marriages for Residency Visas and evidence that the two are living together as a married couple is limited.

Mack's NXIVM business was her non-profit charity called 'Juicy Peach'. The organization was created to promote the arts. However, it failed after no funding sources materialized. Mack and Kreuk originally designed a calendar and sold it online. However, all proceeds were returned as the duo could not complete and ship the calendar.

In a strange twist of fate, the Juicy Peach logo (hand-drawn and designed by Mack), looks like an upside-down vagina with a bite mark. The bite mark, dripping blood, is the same spot where her slaves would be branded ten years later, with the initials KR and AM for Keith Raniere and Allison Mack.

CLARE BRONFMAN
Alias: THE ENFORCER

Sex: Female
Race: White
DOB: 4/8/1979
POB: New York, NY
Height: 5' 7"
Weight: 90
Eyes: Brown
Hair: Black
BOP Number: None Yet Assigned

Alleged Crimes: Obstruction of Justice (witness tampering), Bulk Cash Smuggling, Tax Evasion

Background: Clare grew up in England and Kenya, with her mother Rita Webb, and has a slight British accent. Her educational background is unknown. No one knows if Clare has a High School diploma or equivalent. No college work is shown.

Clare promotes herself as a World Class equestrian. However, she has only placed in low-level riding events with only one podium finish. Her sole championship came at the amateur level CSI-A (lowest tier with $5,000 purse) riding competition. At her self-proclaimed peak, she says she was ranked 80th in the World, but no one can verify this ranking.

Clare became involved in NXIVM in 2004, having completed a course in Monterrey, Mexico. Clare was quickly recognized as a source of income and funding for the organization, due to her status as daughter of Seagrams billionaire owner Edgar Bronfman, Sr. Clare has access to a large trust fund and has funded NXIVM (and the business plans of Keith Raniere and Nancy Salzman) to the tune of over $100 Million dollars.

Clare is also known as the Enforcer of the enterprise, as it is alleged she hired Private Investigators, former CIA agents, attorneys, researchers, and consultants to conduct character assassinations and file lawsuits against anyone that would question NXIVM. In the past, such targets have included Toni Natalie, Barbara Bouchey, Frank Parlato, and former Albany Times Union reporter James Oderno. Clare also makes considerable donations to local politicians in the Albany County area, hence NXIVM has been able to operate nearly 20 years without law enforcement action, despite countless criminal complaints about NXIVM to local authorities. Clare has also funded national politicians including the Clinton campaign and Clinton foundation. Clare also hired senior Republican Strategist and lobbyist Roger Stone as a consultant.

It is unknown whether or not Clare participated in obstruction of justice and witness tampering. Based on FBI reports and eyewitness statements, it is alleged that Clare hired an attorney in Mexico to send cease-and-desist letters to government witnesses and NXIVM defectors. It is also alleged that someone paid money to a judge in Mexico, so that arrest warrants would be issued for these same witnesses and defectors. The purpose was to have the witnesses and defectors thrown into Mexican jails. It is unknown whether or not Clare participated in this scheme.

It is unknown whether or not Clare (or someone acting on her behalf) also purchased several websites meant to intimidate Federal witnesses including _____ exposed.com. The 'blank' represents the name of the witness such as frankparlatoexposed.com and markvicenteexposed.com. This is also obstruction of justice and witness tampering.

It is unknown whether or not Clare participated in bulk cash smuggling. Based on FBI reports and eyewitnesses, a jet was used to smuggle cash from NXIVM training centers in Mexico City and Monterrey, Mexico to Albany, New York. When FBI agents searched the home of Nancy Salzman, more than $500,000 in USD cash was found hidden in boxes. The currency also included Mexican pesos and Russian rubles.

It is unknown whether or not Clare participated in income tax evasion. Based on FBI reports and eyewitness statements, it is alleged that someone aided Nancy Salzman to create shell companies and non-profit organizations in order to launder money from Mexico and/or to recharacterize contributions to NXIVM as tax-free earnings.

In addition, Keith Raniere claims to be a pauper, yet more than $8 Million dollars was found in his checking account. If someone assisted Keith to avoid paying federal income taxes on gifts or consultant fees as a source of income, this would be conspiracy to commit income tax evasion.

WARNING: Approach with EXTREME caution. Clare Bronfman has access to millions of dollars and in the past has allegedly used muscle including former CIA contractors, private investigators, bodyguards, and attorneys to silence and intimidate defectors from NXIVM.

SARA BRONFMAN
Alias: THE PARTYGIRL, BLONDIE

Sex: Female
Race: White
DOB: 1976
POB: Unknown
Height: 5' 7"
Weight: 120
Eyes: Blue
Hair: Blonde

Alleged Crimes: Unknown

Background: Sara grew up in England and Kenya with her mother Rita Webb, and her sister Clare. Sara is shy, soft-spoken, and withdrawn. Her educational background is unknown. No college work is shown.

Sara began taking NXIVM and ESP courses in 2001. Sara was identified as a source of revenue for the organization and groomed because she 'didn't ask too many questions.' The humanitarian cloak of NXIVM attracted Sara to become more and more involved. Sara was promoted to the position of head trainer and responsible for several high-profile NXIVM events, including trips to Sir Richard Branson's Necker Island and the Dalai Lama's visit to Albany, New York in 2009.

It is unknown at this time, how much of the day-to-day structure of NXIVM was managed and/or run by Sara Bronfman. It is not a crime to squander a large inheritance. Of the two sisters, Clare Bronfman was allegedly more involved in the operational and financial aspects of NXIVM than Sara.

It is unknown whether either of the two Bronfman sisters ever questioned Keith Raniere on some of his unbelievable claims (high IQ and physical prowess) and his lack of personal ethics. It is believed that Clare Bronfman and Nancy Salzman are more rivals, than co-workers.

KRISTIN LAURA KREUK
Alias: THE FACE OF NXIVM, STAR RECRUITER

Sex: Female
Race: White, Asian
DOB: 12/30/1982
POB: Vancouver, BC
Height: 5' 5"
Weight: 105
Eyes: Brown
Hair: Brown

Background: Kristin Kreuk grew up in Vancouver, BC.
She is the daughter of two landscape architects, Peter
Kreuk and Deanna Che. Kreuk was selected in High
School to audition for the role of Lana Lang in the
Vancouver-produced hit CW TV Series *Smallville*. Kreuk
was cast before the lead, Tom Welling.

Kreuk was recruited into NXIVM in 2006 and would
appear as the face of NXIVM for several events,
including Acapella Innovations and other recruitment

drives. Although Kreuk denies she was a senior member, Kreuk was involved in numerous NXIVM high-level meetings held on Sir Richard Branson's Necker Island. Kreuk was also groomed by Nancy Salzman to be an ambassador for NXIVM and ESP due to Kreuk's fame and notoriety. Kreuk also recruited many of her close friends into NXIVM including Allison Mack, Kendra Voth, Sima Kumar, and others.

Kreuk's NXIVM business was Girls by Design. The company was supposed to promote teen female empowerment and leadership through workshops and weekend escapes. However, the company folded after several years due to lack of interest and funding. Kreuk would also have meetings for NXIVM, JNess (another NXIVM organization), and Girls by Design in her home.

Although Kreuk attempted to downplay her role in NXIVM via a statement released in 2018, it is alleged she was heavily involved in recruitment, coaching, staffing, and leadership. As a coach, Kreuk would drive for 4 hours on early Saturday mornings from Vancouver, BC to Tacoma, WA to give lessons. At these lessons, Kreuk was described as tired-looking, incoherent, and lacking personal hygiene with unwashed hair, and unshaved legs and armpits.

Kreuk also self-promotes in the NXIVM mold, providing career highlights that cannot be verified. Although Kreuk claims to have taken 'some college courses', no one can verify these courses and it is believed that she is referring to her NXIVM and ESP classes. In addition, Kreuk self-promotes as a successful businesswoman, yet she doesn't own any businesses except for the failed NXIVM business Girls by Design. Lastly, Kreuk claims to be a feminist, yet she sent many women into an abusive cult, including one of her best friends Allison Mack.

MARK HILDRETH
Alias: THE GATEKEEPER, THE SOURCE

Sex: Male
Race: White
DOB: 1/24/1978
POB: Vancouver, BC
Height: 5' 8"
Weight: 180
Eyes: Brown
Hair: Brown

Alleged Crimes: Immigration/VISA fraud, Income Tax
Evasion

Background: Mark Hildreth was raised by his
grandparents and had his start in the entertainment
industry at age 7. Hildreth is a graduate of the National

Theatre School of Canada. His first acting role was in *Love is Never Silent* in 1985.

Hildreth was recruited into NXIVM in 2004. He was quickly identified as a source who could be used to recruit and turn additional actors to NXIVM, to provide the organization with more legitimacy and acceptance. Hildreth in turn, recruited his then-girlfriend Kristin Kreuk and others.

For years, Hildreth was a head trainer in the NXIVM organization, giving classes and coaching sessions in the USA and Canada. Since he is in the USA on a work

VISA, he must follow all Federal laws while in the United States. Hildreth was paid for his recruitment efforts and coaching for NXIVM (due to the pyramid scheme nature of NXIVM). If Hildreth did not declare this income to the IRS or Canada Revenue Agency, this would be income tax evasion and a violation of his US VISA.

kr CONVERSATIONS
nformal thoughts on civilization, ethics & humanity.

Mark Hildreth

Biography

Mark Hildreth is an actor and musician liv Vancouver Canada. He has appeared in o' over productions over a 30 year career. He television series The Tudors on Showtime, recipient of the Jessie Richardson Award prestigious National Theater School Of Ca singer/songwriter, has released two origir Canada. He co-stars in the upcoming feat

Although Hildreth distanced himself from NXIVM in 2018, he was heavily involved in programs geared to recruiting and training actors including 'The Source'. In webpages for *The Source* (another NXIVM-created program, as identified in FBI reports), Hildreth is listed as the 'Head Trainer' and 'Leader of the 12-week program'. Hildreth also appears in several videos praising cult leader Keith Raniere and looking upon Raniere with adoring eyes and nervous adulation.

BONUS MATERIALS

FBI AFFIDAVIT TO ARREST KEITH RANIERE

Date: 14 Feb 2018

From: Special Agent Michael Lever
To: Hon. Lois Bloom, U.S. Magistrate Judge, Eastern District of New York

The source of your deponent's information and the grounds for his belief are as follows:

1. I am a Special Agent with the Federal Bureau of Investigation ("FBI") and have been involved in the investigation of cases involving sex trafficking and civil rights violations.

2. I have personally participated in the investigation of the offenses discussed below. The information set forth in this Complaint and Affidavit in Support of Arrest Warrant is derived from my participation in the investigation as well as from, among other things, a review of other records, emails, and reports from other law enforcement agents involved in the investigation. In particular, the FBI has interviewed eight victims and many additional first-hand witnesses to the events described herein, electronic evidence recovered from the victims and witnesses, and the results of several search warrants including one executed on an email account belonging to RANIERE. Because this affidavit is submitted only to establish probable cause to arrest, I

have not included each and every fact known to me concerning this investigation. I have set forth only the facts I believe are necessary to establish probable cause. In addition, when I refer below to the statements of others, such references are in sum and substance and in part.

I. Background

3. In or about 1998, the defendant KEITH RANIERE, also known as "The Vanguard," founded Executive Success Programs, Inc. ("ESP"), a series of workshops designed, according to its promotional literature, to "actualize human potential." In or about 2003, RANIERE founded an organization called Nxivm (pronounced NEX-i-um), which served as an umbrella organization for ESP and other RANIERE-affiliated entities.

4. On its official website, Nxivm is described as a "professional business providing educational tools, coaching and trainings to corporations and people from all walks of life," and describes its philosophy as "a new ethical understanding" that allows "humanity to rise to its noble possibility."

5. Nxivm is headquartered in Albany, New York. Nxivm operates centers all over the Americas including in the United States, Canada, Central America and Mexico. RANIERE and many members of Nxivm ("Nxians") live approximately 20 miles outside of Albany, New York, in Clifton Park, New York, near Nxivm's headquarters. A number of Nxians were res idents of the Eastern District

of New York, when they were recruited, and Nxivm has held promotional recruiting events in Brooklyn, New York.

6. Each of the RANIERE entities offers classes promising personal and professional development. Based on information obtained during the course of this investigation, classes offered by RANIERE-affiliated entities can cost up to $5,000 for a five-day workshop. Participants are encouraged to keep attending classes and to recruit others into the organization in order to rise within the ranks of Nxivm and to reach certain" goal levels." These levels are marked by different color sashes, which are worn by Nxians, as well as different responsibilities and privileges, including the ability to receive a salary or commissions. Many Nxians find themselves in debt from the courses they are required to take, and some are obliged to take jobs working for Nxivm in order to continue taking courses and ostensibly to pay off the ir debts. However, because of the high price of the courses and the pressure to continue taking them, participants often would continue to accumulate new debts and remain obliged to Nxivm.

7. Nxivm operates largely in secrecy. Nxians were often required to sign non-disclosure agreements and to make promises not to reveal certain things about Nxivm's teachings.

8. Nxivm maintains features of a multilevel marketing scheme, commonly known as a pyramid scheme, in which members are recruited via a promise of payments or services for enrolling others into the scheme.

RANIERE formerly ran a multilevel marketing scheme called Consumers Buyline, which was forced to close after a settlement
with the New York Attorney Genera l in 1997, approximately one year before ESP was founded.

9. RANIERE is referred to as "The Vanguard" by Nxians. Every year in August, Nxians pay $2,000 or more to gather in Silver Bay, New York to celebrate "Vanguard Week" in honor of RANIERE, whose birthday is August 26, 1960.

10. Based on information obtained during the course of this investigation, since ESP's founding, RANIERE has maintained a rotating group of fifteen to twenty women with whom he maintains sexual relationships. These women are not permitted to have sexual relationships with anyone but RANIERE or to discuss with others their relationships with RANIERE. Some of the Nxivm curriculum included teachings about the need for men to have multiple sexual partners and the need for women to be monogamous.

II. DOS

A. Founding and Structure

11. In or about 2015, a secret society was developed within Nxivm called "DOS" or the "Vow" (collectively "DOS").

12. DOS is an organized criminal group that operates in

the Eastern District of New York and other parts of the United States, Canada and Mexico. DOS engages in and its activities affect, interstate and foreign commerce.

13. DOS operates as a pyramid with levels of "slaves" headed by "masters." Slaves are expected to recruit slaves of their own (thus becoming masters themselves), who in turn owe service not only to their own masters but also to masters above them in the DOS pyramid.

14. Based on information gathered over the course of this investigation, including RANIERE's own admissions and emails between RANIERE and other members of DOS, RANIERE alone forms the top of the pyramid as the highest master. Other than RANIERE, all participants in DOS are women. RANIERE's status as head of the pyramid was concealed from all newly recruited slaves, other than those directly under RANIERE.

B. Recruiting and Collateral

15. From the time of its inception through in or about Spring 2017, DOS masters recruited slaves mostly from within Nxivm's ranks. When identifying prospective slaves, masters often targeted women who were currently experiencing difficulties in their lives, including dissatisfaction with the pace of their advancement in Nxivm. While avoiding the words "master" and "slave" in the initial recruiting pitch, a master would tell her prospective slave that the prospective slave had an opportunity to join an organization that would change her life. The master then told the prospective slave that, in order to learn more, she had to provide "collateral,"

which was meant to ensure that the prospective slave would keep what she was about to learn a secret. Collateral consisted of material or information that the prospective slave would not want revealed because it would be ruinous to the prospective slave herself and/or someone close to her.

16. Collateral provided by prospective slaves included sexually explicit photographs; videos made to look candid in which the prospective slaves told damning stories (true or untrue) about themselves, close friends and/or family members; and letters making damaging accusations (true or untrue) against friends and family members. In many cases, the masters helped the prospective slaves develop ideas for what would be appropriate collateral or instructed the prospective slaves on lies to tell in order to make the collateral even more damaging.

17. After prospective slaves provided collateral in order to learn more about the organization, the masters informed them that DOS was a women-only organization (RANIERE's role as the highest master was not mentioned) and that the goal of DOS was to eradicate weaknesses in its members. The Nxivm curriculum taught that women had inherent weaknesses including "overemotional" natures, an inability to keep promises and embracing the role of victim. The masters also told prospective slaves that their respective relationships would be of "masters" and "slaves," using those words. If prospective slaves expressed hesitation about the program or about becoming "slaves" and having "masters," the masters downplayed the terms, saying that

all women are slaves to various things. In many cases, masters also used Nxivm techniques to manipulate the prospective slaves into believing that any hesitation to join was due to weaknesses on the part of the prospective slaves and that the hesitation itself was evidence of why they needed DOS.

18. Prospective slaves who agreed to join DOS were told that in order to join they had to provide additional collateral, similar in type to the collateral they had already provided. Some slaves were told that they had to collateralize all aspects of their lives, including signing over any assets, disclaiming their faith, and doing things that would ruin their careers and relationships if the collateral were released. DOS slaves understood that if they left DOS, spoke publicly about DOS, or repeatedly failed DOS obligations or assignments, their collateral could be released.

19. All DOS slaves were ultimately required to provide collateral beyond what had initially been described to them. For example, most DOS slaves were not initially told that they would have to provide collateral evely month. In most cases the DOS slaves continued to provide additional collateral beyond what they had initially under stood was expected, in part because they feared that the collateral they had already provided would be released.

C. Benefits Conferred on DOS Masters

20. DOS slaves were required to perform "acts of care" for their masters and to pay "tribute" to their masters in

various ways. In many cases these acts of care and tribute were akin to acting as personal assistants to the masters - bringing them coffee, buying them groceries, making them lunch, carrying their luggage, cleaning their houses and retrieving lost items for them, among other tasks. The understanding among DOS members was that acts of care provided by a master's slaves, and those slaves' own slaves, should ultimately amount to the master having the work of at least one full time employee.

21. Slaves were chastised and punished for not performing sufficient acts of care, and slaves believed that if they repeatedly failed at acts of care they risked release of their collateral.

D. Sex Trafficking Within DOS

22. Beyond acts of care, DOS slaves were also regularly given assignments to complete by their masters. Some of the masters gave their slaves assignments that either directly or implicitly required them to have sex with RANIERE, which they then did. Other assignments appeared designed to groom slaves sexually for RANIERE. For example, RANIERE is known to sexually prefer women who are exceptionally thin, and a number of the slaves' assignments required them to adhere to extremely low-calorie diets and to document every food they ate. Other women were assigned to periods of celibacy, during which they were not allowed to have sex with anyone or masturbate.

23. Based on information obtained over the course of the investigation, DOS victims who received the assignment

to have sex with RANIERE believed they had to complete the assignment or risk release of their collateral.

24. The DOS masters, including Co-Conspirator 1 ("CC-1," described below), who directed their slaves to have sex with RANIERE profited from the resulting sex acts. Those DOS masters received a financial benefit in the form of continued status and participation in DOS, i.e. the masters continued to receive acts of care and the work of the equivalent of a full-time employee. In addition, by requiring DOS slaves to have sex with RANIERE, DOS masters also received benefits from RANIERE in the form of increased status and financial opportunities within Nxivm more broadly. RANIERE also often discussed or promised career opportunities to the DOS slaves who had sex with him and the DOS slaves with whom he expressed an interest in having sex. As one example, discussed further below, once Jane Doe 1 began having sex with RANIERE, he provided her with money and offered her a job, but as soon as she defected from DOS and stopped having sex with him, RANIERE told her she had to pay the money back.

E. Other Assignments and "Readiness"

25. DOS slaves were also regularly given assignments to complete by their masters that included reviewing ESP materials and doing other work for Nxivm or RANIERE. This work included reviewing and editing dense articles written by RANIERE and, at least in one case described further below, transcribing interviews of a high-ranking member of Nxivm for a memorial service being hosted by RANIERE.

26. In addition to completing acts of care and assignments, DOS slaves were required to participate in "readiness" drills. The purpose of these drills was to have everyone in the DOS pyramid respond by text message at any given time of the day or night. Readiness drills along with other aspects of the DOS program resulted in the slaves suffering from severe sleep deprivation.

27. DOS slaves also had to engage in acts of self-denial or acts that would cause them discomfort, including taking ice cold showers for several minutes, standing for an hour at 4:00 a.m. and performing planks (a difficult exercise where one rests on her forearms and tiptoes and keeps her back as flat as possible).

28. Based on information obtained over the course of the investigation, DOS victims have explained that they believed they had to complete their assignments and comply with readiness drills and acts of self-denial or risk release of their collateral. Additionally, several DOS victims believed that their success in the Nxivm ranking system depended on their successfully completing DOS assignments.

29. Furthermore, masters informed their slaves that if the slaves failed to complete their assignments, it reflected badly on the masters and could cause them to be punished by their own masters. In at least one instance, a master who, unbeknownst to her slaves, was herself a direct slave of RANIERE's, told her slaves that she could be punished by being paddled or by being put in a cage

by her master, i.e. by RANIERE, for her slaves' failure to succeed at "readiness."

F. Branding

30. Many of the DOS victims were branded in their pubic regions with a cauterizing pen in a process that took twenty to thirty minutes. During the branding "ceremonies," slaves were required to be fully naked, and the master would order one slave to film while the others held down the slave being branded. Some DOS victims were told that the brand stood for the four elements (the lines represented air, earth and water and the cauterizing pen represented sealing with fire). Based on information obtained during the course of the investigation, however, it is clear that the brand in fact consisted of RANIERE's initials. After defections, discussed below in paragraph 33, RANIERE acknowledged to one DOS victim that his initials are incorporated into the brand as a form of "tribute."

31. Masters told their slaves after the branding ceremonies that the videos of the branding ceremonies and photographs of the women with their brands were additional pieces of collateral.

32. The first image below is a picture of victim Jane Doe 1's brand as it appeared on her body shortly after the procedure. The second image shows the brand turned counter-clockwise with RANIERE's initials (the "R" upside down) superimposed.

III. Defections and Aftermath

33. In or about May 20 17, a DOS slave (who was also a high-ranking member of Nxivm) defected in a public way. At that time, Nxians began learning about the existence of DOS and there' was some defection of Nxians, including a member of the Executive Board and additional DOS members.

34. In or about October 2017, the New York Times published an article revealing the existence of DOS. Several weeks after that a l l icle was published and after the FBI began interviewing witnesses, RANIERE flew to Mexico with an heiress (the "Heiress"), who is a member of Nxivm's Executive Board and is a known financial backer of RANIERE and Nxivm. Prior to this trip, RANIERE had not flown out of the country since 2015, when he visited the Heiress's private island in Fiji. RANIERE is currently believed to be residing in Monterrey, Mexico, where Nxivm maintains a center, with a branded DOS slave.

35. Since defecting, several DOS victims have received "cease and desist" letters from a Mexican attorney. Emails exchanged between RANIERE and the Heiress, received pursuant to a search warrant executed on RANIERE's email account, discussed below, reveal that the Heiress and RANIERE orchestrated the sending of those letters. Additionally, the Heiress has made multiple attempts to have criminal charges brought against a former DOS slave, who has discussed her experience in the media.

IV. Yahoo! Email Account

36. On January 18, 2018, Eastern District of New York United States Magistrate Judge Chery l Pollak signed a search warrant for Yahoo! e-mail account keithraniere@yahoo .com (the "account") . I served the warrant on Yahoo! on January 19, 2018. On February 1, 2018, Yahoo! produced information associated with the account. The subscriber for the account was identified as "Mr Keith Raniere." The subscriber information also included a date of birth that matched that of RANIERE .

37. Within the material provided by Yahoo! were numerous emails, only a few of which are described here, which support the conclusion that RANIERE created DOS. On August 10, 2015, CC-1 sent an email to the account. CC-1's email was titled "vow 3" and included an attached letter. The letter pledged CC-1's "full and complete life" to RANIERE. In the letter, CC-1 used the terms "slave" and "master" to refer to herself and RANIERE. Moreover, the letter identified "collateral" to "cement" the vow made by CC-1. This collateral was described as: (1) a letter regarding CC-1's mother and father that would "destroy their character"; (2) a contract that transferred custody of any children birthed by CC-1 to RANIERE if CC-1 broke her commitment to RANIERE; (3) a contract that transferred ownership of CC-1's home if the commitment to RANIERE was broken; and (4) a letter addressed to social services alleging abuse to CC-1's nephews.

38. On July 12, 2015, another woman believed to be a DOS master directly under RANIERE, sent an email to

another email account believed to belong to RANIERE, which RANIERE then forwarded to the account. In the email, the woman requested edits from RANIERE to a series of passages in which she described a vow of total obedience to RANIERE.

39. The account also contained emails between another woman believed to be a DOS slave and RANIERE. Attached to some of the emails were WhatsApp chats between the woman and RANIERE. These chats include discussions from as early as in or about May 2015 about a "vow " that required "collateral." On or about, October 1, 2015, RANIERE stated to the woman, "I think it would be good for you to own a fuck toy slave for me, that you could groom, and use as a tool, to pleasure me.... " On or about, October 23, 2015, RANIERE again suggested the woman recruit a slave who would seduce RANIERE. Throughout the chat RANIERE alludes to the fact that DOS was his creation.

V. Co-Conspirators

40. CC-1 is an actress and is currently understood to be one of the women with whom RANIERE maintained a sexual relationship prior to the development of DOS. Statements on Nxivm-related websites, including video interviews of RANIERE and CC-1, refer to RANIERE' s mentorship of CC-1, and to RANIERE' s and CC-1 's co-development of "The Source," a Nxivm-affiliated entity focused on improving actors' performance skills. Based on information obtained over the course of the investigation, including admissions by RANIERE and

emails between RANIERE and CC-1, CC-1 is RANIERE's direct slave.

41. Co-Conspirator 2 ("CC-2") had been involved in Nxivm for several years before being introduced to DOS. In or about 2016, RANIERE co-founded "The Delegates" with CC-2, which is a business that provides a network of people who can perform tasks for people in the Nxivm community in exchange for a fee. Based on information obtained over the course of the investigation, CC-2 is CC-1's direct slave.

VI. Sex Trafficking and Forced Labor of Jane Doe

42. Jane Doe 1 is an actress in her early thirties who began taking Nxivm classes in or about 2015, including The Source classes with CC-1. In or about February 2016, CC-1 invited Jane Doe 1 to join a "women's mentorship group," but asked that Jane Doe 1 first provide collateral. At CC-1's direction, Jane Doe 1 wrote letters detailing false and highly damaging accusations against her family members. Once Jane Doe 1 had provided this collateral, CC-1 told her about DOS, referring to it as "The Vow."

43. Jane Doe 1 agreed to become CC-1's slave, provided more collateral (eventually including her credit card numbers with letters granting CC-1 permission to use the numbers to make charges) and began receiving assignments. Throughout her time in DOS, Jane Doe 1 was living in Brooklyn, New York. CC-1 ordered Jane Doe 1 to travel to Clifton Park nearly every week from

Brooklyn. When Jane Doe 1 was in Clifton Park, she stayed with CC-1 and CC-2, another of CC-1's slaves.

44. CC-1 told Jane Doe 1 that Jane Doe 1 had to be celibate for six months. Eventually, Jane Doe 1 began receiving assignments that involved contact with RANIERE. At first CC-1 tasked Jane Doe 1 with getting RANIERE to send Jane Doe 1 an email, which she eventually succeeded at doing. One night when Jane Doe 1 was staying with CC-1 in Clifton Park, CC-1 received a text message from RANIERE, woke Jane Doe 1 in the middle of the night, and told her that RANIERE was there to go on a walk with her. CC-1 told Jane Doe 1 that Jane Doe 1 was assigned to tell RANIERE that Jane Doe 1 would do anything RANIERE asked her to do. Jane Doe 1 did as she was ordered and RANIERE asked her what the worst thing he could order her to do was. Jane Doe 1 told RANIERE that she had initially thought it would be something sexual, but that the worst thing would be if he asked her to kill herself or someone else. At the end of the walk, RANIERE told Jane Doe 1 that he did not believe she really meant she would do anything he asked.

45. The next night CC-1 again received a text message from RANIERE, woke Jane Doe 1 in the middle of the night and assigned her to meet RANIERE and tell him she would do anything he asked her to do. Jane Doe 1 did as she was assigned, and RANIERE led her to a house across the street. RANIERE directed her to remove all her clothes and made comments about her naked body. RANIERE then blindfolded Jane Doe 1, led her into a car and drove her around in a manner that made Jane Doe 1

believe RANIERE was trying to prevent her from knowing where they were going. RANIERE led Jane Doe 1, still blindfolded, through some trees, into what she believed was a shack, and tied her to a table. Another person in the room, who Jane Doe 1 did not previously know was present, began performing oral sex on Jane Doe 1 as RANJERE circled the table making comments. Jane Doe 1 did not want to participate in this sexual activity, but believed it was part of her commitment to DOS and that if she broke her commitment to DOS her collateral could be released.

46. Jane Doe 1 was never put on a diet by CC-1, but Jane Doe 1 was 5 '5" tall and weighed only 100 pounds before joining DOS, and she then lost some additional weight as a member of DOS due to stress and lack of sleep.

47. In the following months, RANIERE had repeated sexual contact with Jane Doe 1, including oral sex and sexual intercourse on a number of occasions. He would take her to a space he called the "Library," which was on the second floor of a house in Clifton Park (the first floor was under construct ion). The Library had a hot tub and a loft bed. RANIERE told Jane Doe 1 that he was CC-1's master and Jane Doe 1's "grandmaster." RANIERE told Jane Doe 1 that he had conceived the concept of DOS. RANIERE explained to Jane Doe 1 that he could order her to have sex with him, although he claimed that was not what he was doing. Jane Doe 1 felt, however, that having sex with RANIERE was paid of her DOS commitment and that if she broke her commitment to DOS, her collateral might be released.

48. Jane Doe 1 believed that at some point all the other slaves directly under CC-1, which included CC-2, learned that RANIERE was CC-1's master and their grandmaster. Throughout Jane Doe 1's time in DOS, CC-1 regularly required her slaves to pose for nude photographs, including on one occasion close-up pictures of their vaginas, either as assignments or collateral. Jane Doe 1 later learned that CC-1 was sending these photographs to RANIERE, because Jane Doe 1 observed CC-1 sending these photographs using CC-1's cellphone to someone over a messaging service and then receiving responses which CC-1 would sometimes relay to her slaves. The responses included that the photographs were not graphic enough or that the slaves were not smiling enough, and that they had to be retaken. On one occasion, Jane Doe 1 saw a text exchange on CC-1's phone between RANIERE and CC-1, in which CC-1 sent a nude photo she had just taken of all of the slaves on Jane Doe 1's level and RANIERE wrote back, "All mine?" with a smiling devil emoji.

49. At one point, Jane Doe 1 expressed to RANIERE that she was having difficulty affording the frequent trips to Clifton Park. RANIERE was frustrated with her and took a bag with $10,000 in cash from a drawer in the Library and asked! her if that would make her happy. Jane Doe 1 began using the cash to pay for her trips, only taking enough for the ticket each time she visited. On one occasion when she needed money, RANIERE gave her $1,000 from the bag. Jane Doe 1 also occasionally expressed frustration at having to be celibate and only be sexual with RANIERE, and RANIERE would encourage her to wait a year, which gave Jane Doe 1 some hope that

although she could not leave then, she might be able to leave in a year without risking release of her collateral. Jane Doe 1 stated that when she would bring up the one-year period with RANIERE, he would frequently change the date on which he said the year started.

50. As part of her DOS assignments, Jane Doe 1 was tasked by CC-1 with reading and reviewing dense articles written by RANIERE that were labeled at the bottom with ESP's copyright. Each artic le took hours to review and Jane Doe 1 was tasked with reviewing up to approximately 95 articles. Jane Doe 1 was required to fill out a standardized form after reading each article, which appeared designed to determine whether the articles were appropriate to include in the ESP curriculum or if there were further edits that needed to be made in order for them to be useful to students. Jane Doe 1 also received an assignment from CC-1 to transcribe interviews given by a long-term sexual partner of RANIERE's, who had died, in preparation for that woman's memorial service. Jane Doe 1 was awake for 23 hours straight completing that project, and RANIERE exchanged messages with her throughout the night encouraging her to stay awake and complete the assignment.

RANIERE also directly tasked Jane Doe 1 with an assignment to befriend and learn information about an ostracized member of the ESP/Nxivm community. As part of this plan, RANIERE directed Jane Doe 1 to make a false social media profile and eventually to meet this ostracized member of the community in person. Jane Doe 1 believed that each one of these assignments was part of her commitment to DOS and that if she failed at her commitment to DOS, her collateral could be released.

51. After the May 2017 incident, as described in paragraph 33, because other DOS members had left without having had (to Jane Doe 1's knowledge) their collateral released, Jane Doe 1 began to believe she might also be able to leave without having her collateral released. When she told CC-1 and CC-2 that she was leaving DOS, they engaged in a two-hour "intervention," during which Jane Doe 1 was berated for leaving. Throughout the conversation, Jane Doe 1 sought assurances about her collateral. Although CC-1 and CC-2 never directly said her collateral would not be released, she felt assured enough that as long as she did not speak out about DOS (as opposed to just breaking her lifetime commitment), her collateral would not be released. After the intervention, RANIERE met Jane Doe 1 and told her she needed to return the money he had previously given her.

VII. Sex Trafficking of Jane Doe 2

52. Jane Doe 2 is an actress and model who began taking Nxivm classes in or about 2016, during which time she became friendly with CC-2. When Jane Doe 2 was in Clifton Park for a Nxivm class in or about November 2016, CC-2 invited Jane Doe 2 on a walk. As they walked, CC-2 told Jane Doe 2 that she was part of a secret society that had transformed CC-2 's life and enabled CC-2 to uphold CC-2 's commitments. CC-2 told Jane Doe 2 that in order to learn more, Jane Doe 2 had to provide collateral, which Jane Doe 2 did in the form of a

video in which Jane Doe 2 divulged a damaging secret. After providing this video, CC-2 told Jane Doe 2 about DOS and Jane Doe 2 agreed to become CC-2's slave.

53. Eventually CC-2 told Jane Doe 2 that CC-1 was CC-2's master and thus Jane Doe 2's grandmaster. When Jane Doe 2 was introduced to DOS, she was living in Los Angeles, California. After Jane Doe 2 joined DOS, CC-1 suggested that Jane Doe 2 temporarily move to Clifton Park, New York and spend more time with CC- 1 and CC-2. Jane Doe 2 began spending more time in Clifton Park, but regularly traveled back to Los Angeles for jobs. When Jane Doe 2 would travel between Los Angeles and Clifton Park, she would regularly fly into John F. Kennedy International Airport in Queens, New York before taking the train or bus to Albany.

54. Two of Jane Doe 2's first acts of self-denial were to refrain from sex and masturbation.

55. At one point when Jane Doe 2 was in Clifton Park, RANIERE sent Jane Doe 2 a message in the middle of the night asking her to go on a walk with him. During the walk, RANIERE told Jane Doe 2 sexual jokes. Over the course of several walks,
Jane Doe 2 expressed to RANIERE that she wanted to open a T-shirt business. RANIERE expressed interest and told her he would partner with her. Jane Doe 2 left for Los Angeles for a job and while she was there RANIERE sent her a text message saying, "If you want to start this business with me then come back, the sooner the better."

56. Jane Doe 2 returned to Clifton Park. She was soon given new assignments, including being kept on a regimented diet of 860-1000 calories per day. After several months, Jane Doe 2 received a text message from CC-1 stating that CC-1 wanted to speak to Jane Doe 2 about a "special assignment." CC-1 and CC-2 then contacted Jane Doe 2 and told her the assignment was to "seduce Keith" and have him take a picture of Jane Doe 2 to prove she had done it. CC-1 told Jane Doe 2 that this assignment was a privilege that few women had the honor of experiencing, but that CC-1 and CC-2 both had. At the end of the call CC-1 told Jane Doe 2, "I give you permission to enjoy it," which Jane Doe 2 interpreted to mean, "I give you permission to enjoy sex with RANIERE." Not suspecting that RANIERE was involved with DOS until this call, Jane Doe 2 asked CC-1 on the call if RANIERE knew about DOS. CC-1 said that he did not.

57. After the call, in an effort to avoid having sex with RANIERE, Jane Doe 2 made arrangements to leave DOS. Jane Doe 2 retrieved a car that she had loaned to CC-1 and her cat and possessions from Clifton Park. Before defecting, Jane Doe 2 also captured images of collateral belonging to other DOS members, including CC-2, from an online Dropbox account, believing that she could protect the release of her own collateral by having other DOS members' collateral as leverage. Jane Doe 2 officially left DOS in or about May 2016.

WHEREFORE, your deponent respectfully requests that an arrest warrant be issued for the defendant KEITH RANIERE so that he may be dealt with according to law.

Your affiant further requests that this affidavit and any associated arrest warrant be filed under seal, because public filing would give the target of the investigation an opportunity to flee, to destroy evidence and to harm or threaten witnesses.

Signed,

/s/ Michael Lever

MICHAEL LEVER
Special Agent, Federal Bureau of Investigation

LETTER REQUESTING DENIAL OF BOND FOR KEITH RANIERE

Case No: 18-M-132

Date: March 26, 2018

From: US Department of Justice, United States
 Attorney Eastern District of New York

To: Hon. Steven M. Gold, U.S. Magistrate, EDNY

Dear Judge Gold:

The defendant Keith Raniere is scheduled to appear in the Northern District of Texas tomorrow at 2:00 p.m. for arraignment. The government respectfully submits this letter in anticipation of the defendant's expected removal to the Eastern District of New York and in support of the government's request for a permanent order of detention. As set forth below, the defendant, who was living in Mexico prior to his arrest and has access to vast resources, poses a significant risk of flight. In addition, his long-standing history of systematically exploiting women through coercive practices for his own financial and sexual benefit demonstrates that, if released, he would pose a danger to the community.

I. Background

A. Complaint

The defendant is charged by complaint with sex trafficking, sex trafficking conspiracy and conspiracy to commit forced labor. As described in detail in the complaint (the facts of which are incorporated by reference into this letter), these charges arise from the defendant's role as the leader of a secret society called "DOS" or "The Vow," in which women were recruited to be slaves under the false pretense of joining a women-only mentorship group. DOS is structured as a pyramid with the defendant at the top. To join DOS, slaves were required to provide their masters with "collateral," which included highly damaging information about themselves and/or family members, naked photographs and rights to their assets. Once they had joined, slaves learned they had to provide additional collateral, which they did, fearing that otherwise the collateral they had already provided would be used against them. None of the slaves (except for those directly under the defendant) knew that the defendant was involved in the organization when they were recruited.

DOS slaves understood that if they told anyone about DOS, if they left DOS or if they failed to complete assignments given to them by their masters, their collateral could be released. A number of DOS slaves (including Jane Does 1 and 2, as described in the complaint) were given assignments that implicitly or expressly directed them to have sex with the defendant. Moreover, a number of DOS slaves, including Jane Doe 1, performed services other than sex (such as editing the defendant's articles and transcribing interviews) for the benefit of the defendant, believing that if they did not, their collateral could be released. The masters who gave these assignments received the financial benefit of free labor from their slaves. Many DOS slaves were also groomed for sex with the defendant by (1) being ordered to adhere to very restricted diets (the defendant is known to sexually prefer extremely thin women), (2) being ordered to remain celibate (the defendant has taught that women should be monogamous but that men are naturally polyamorous), and/or (3) being ordered to stop waxing or shaving their pubic hair (the defendant is known to sexually prefer women with a lot of pubic hair). The slaves were told that they were being given these orders to benefit themselves. The DOS masters who directed their slaves to have sex with the defendant received financial benefits in the form of continued status and participation in DOS, as well as financial opportunities from the defendant.

DOS slaves were seriously sleep-deprived from participating in "readiness" drills, which required them to respond to their masters any time day or night. DOS slaves were also branded in their pelvic regions with a cauterizing pen with a symbol that, unbeknownst to them, incorporated the defendant's initials.

The government estimates that the defendant has had more than fifty DOS slaves under him.

Many DOS slaves were recruited from Nxivm, which is the umbrella organization for a number of self-help workshops created by the defendant and that have been taught at centers across the country and internationally since 1998. The defendant is revered within Nxivm and referred to as the "Vanguard." Every week in August, the Nxivm community gathers for a week to celebrate the defendant's birthday and pay tribute to him. According to a number of sources, including former high-ranking members of Nxivm, the defendant's word is final within Nxivm and nothing of import happens within Nxivm without the defendant's approval. Nxivm students are also taught that the defendant is the smartest and most ethical man in the world. He frequently cited having earned three degrees from Rensselaer Polytechnic Institute, but a review of his transcript shows that he graduated with a 2.26 GPA, having failed or barely passed many of the upper-level math and science classes he bragged about taking.

Nxivm maintains features of a pyramid scheme, as courses cost thousands of dollars each and participants are encouraged to continue to pay for additional classes and to recruit others to take classes in order to rise within the ranks of Nxivm. Different ranks are marked by different color sashes, and students must reach certain ranks in order to begin receiving salaries or commissions. Members of Nxivm are taught that they can get rich by advancing in Nxivm, but in reality only a small percentage of Nxians make significant income and a much larger percentage find themselves in significant debt to the organization. The defendant had previously been investigated by law enforcement for operating a pyramid scheme called "Consumers' Buyline, Inc." As part of a consent order entered into in 1996 by the defendant and the New York State Attorney General's

Office, the defendant was prohibited from operating a multilevel-marketing scheme in New York again.

B. History of Sexual Assault and Other Abuse of Girls and Women

The defendant has a decades' long history of abusing women and girls. According to confidential sources, the defendant had repeated sexual encounters with multiple teenage girls in the mid-to-late 1980s and early 1990s. In one instance, the defendant met a fifteen-year-old girl while he was in his 20s and had repeated sexual contact with her. In another instance, the defendant met a twelve-year-old girl whose mother worked for the defendant and began tutoring her. Shortly thereafter, the defendant began having regular sexual intercourse with her, including at his home where he lived with multiple adult sexual partners. One of those partners hired the girl to walk her dog, giving the defendant daily access to the girl. The defendant told one of the DOS slaves he had sex with that he believed the age of consent was too rigid and that it should be lowered to when a child's parent says the child is capable of consent.

Furthermore, the defendant directed the abuse of Nxivm members who had committed so-called "ethical breaches." In one instance, the defendant ordered the long-term confinement of a Nxivm member who was approximately in her early-20s to heal an "ethical breach" because she had developed romantic feelings for someone other than him. During her approximately 18-month confinement, with limited exceptions, the woman had extremely limited contact with her family or other members of the community and she received limited medical attention. Her period of confinement was repeatedly extended for other supposed ethical breaches, including, in one instance, because she cut her hair. The woman felt she could not leave because of the repercussions on her family and also because she was illegally in the United States and the defendant and other members of Nxivm had helped her illegally enter.

The defendant has also physically assaulted at least two intimate partners and in 2012, under the guise of mentorship, he encouraged a woman to run headfirst into a tree and to drink from a puddle. He also co-founded a movement called "Society of Protectors," which, in part, relied on humiliating women in order to eradicate weaknesses the defendant taught were common in women. For example, women attending the classes were forced to wear fake cow udders over their breasts while people called them derogatory names. Moreover, at least one DOS master who was directly under the defendant told her slaves that her own master, i.e., the defendant, would put her in a cage to punish her.

The defendant has also posed disturbing hypotheticals as part of the Nxivm curriculum, challenging whether incest and rape are actually wrong. He told one DOS slave that incest is not wrong if the "victim" is sexually aroused by the experience, and he questioned whether gang rape is bad if the person being raped has an orgasm.

C. Defendant's Foreign Ties and Access to Cash

For most of his life the defendant has lived outside

Albany, New York, where Nxivm is headquartered.
Many members of Nxivm live in the same area. Shortly
after the government began interviewing witnesses and
victims in November 2017, the defendant flew to
Mexico. For over a month and a half, since the arrest
warrant in this case was issued, the government has
actively worked with Mexican immigration officials to
locate the defendant. Finding the defendant was difficult
because the defendant purposely concealed his location,
began using end-to-end encrypted email and stopped
using his phone. Ultimately, the defendant was found to
be staying at a luxury villa near Puerto Vallarta, Mexico
with several women. The villa was in a gated community
where some villas cost over $10,000 U.S.C. a week to
rent. The defendant was uncooperative when immigration
authorities arrived and after he was taken into custody,
the women chased the car in which the defendant was
being transported in their own car at high speed.

The defendant pretends to be a renunciate. In reality,
however, he has spent his life profiting from his pyramid
schemes and has otherwise received financial backing
from independently wealthy women. The defendant is
currently financially backed by Clare Bronfman, an
heiress to the Seagram's liquor fortune. She has financed
the defendant repeatedly over the years including
providing him with millions of dollars and paying for
private air travel costing up to approximately $65,000 a
flight. She has also paid for numerous lawyers to bring
suits against Nxivm critics. Bronfman also owns a private
island in Fiji, which the defendant has visited, and both
Bronfman and the defendant have contacts all around the
world.

The defendant does not keep any money in his name and has no driver's license. He makes purchases using a credit card in one of his dead lover's names. In the past year and a half, the defendant and the mother of his child have accessed hundreds of thousands of dollars from a bank account in the same dead lover's name, which contains over $8 million dollars.

D. Past Obstruction

According to multiple confidential sources, in connection with a civil action brought in the District of New Jersey against cult critic Rick Ross and others that was dismissed this year, the defendant directed several members of Nxivm to edit video recordings of Nxivm classes that Nxivm had been ordered to produce in discovery. The edits removed portions of the classes that the defendant thought would be damaging to Nxivm's case.

In addition, since defecting, several DOS victims have received "cease and desist" letters from a Mexican attorney. As set forth in the complaint, the defendant was involved in sending those letters.

II. Legal Standard

Under the Bail Reform Act, Title 18, United States Code, Sections 3141, et seq. (the "Act"), federal courts "shall" order a defendant's detention pending trial upon a determination that "no condition or combination of conditions would reasonably assure the appearance of the person as required and the safety of any other person and the community[.]" 18 U.S.C. § 3142(e). A finding of risk of dangerousness must be supported by clear and convincing evidence and a finding of risk of flight must be supported by a preponderance of the evidence. See *United States v. Chimurenga,* 760 F.2d 400, 405 (2d Cir. 1985).

Whether detention is sought on the basis of flight or dangerousness, the Bail Reform Act lists four factors to be considered in the detention analysis:

(1) "the nature and circumstances of the offense charged. . .";

(2) "the weight of the evidence against the person";

(3) "the history and characteristics of the person, including . . . the person's character, . . . past conduct, . . . [and] criminal history, and record concerning appearance at court proceedings"; and

(4) "the nature and seriousness of the danger to any person or the community that would be posed by the person's release."

See 18 U.S.C. § 3142(g).

The concept of "dangerousness" encompasses not only the effect of a defendant's release on the safety of identifiable individuals, such as victims and witnesses, but also "'the danger that the defendant might engage in criminal activity to the detriment of the community.'"

United States v. Millan, 4 F.3d 1038, 1048 (2d Cir. 1993) (quoting legislative history). In addition – and significantly – when a finding of dangerousness is related to violent conduct, it need not be shown that the defendant personally engaged in violence. *United States v. Colombo,* 777 F.2d 96, 98 (2d Cir. 1985).

Moreover, the Second Circuit has held that "prior acts of domestic violence are relevant to a determination of dangerousness" because a "willingness to strike loved ones offers probative evidence of tendency to violence and dangerousness towards others." *United States v. Mercedes,* 354 F.3d 433, 4337-38 (2d Cir. 2001).

The government is entitled to proceed by proffer in detention hearings. *United States v. LaFontaine,* 210 F.3d 125, 130-31 (2d Cir. 2000).

III. Argument

The nature of the charges outlined in the complaint demonstrates that the defendant poses a significant risk of flight and danger to the community. The defendant is charged with sex trafficking and conspiracy to commit forced labor in a scheme involving over fifty female slaves he directed others to recruit on his behalf. He is charged with trafficking these women through coercion and manipulation, tactics that he has used before.

After law enforcement began interviewing witnesses about the defendant's criminal conduct, he fled to Mexico where he was apprehended only after a month-and-a-half of active searching. The defendant began using encrypted email and stopped using the phone that had been known to law enforcement shortly after the government began interviewing witnesses.

The defendant faces a mandatory minimum sentence of 15 years' imprisonment and an approximate Guidelines range of at least 188 to 235 months' imprisonment on the sex trafficking charge alone. The Second Circuit has held that the possibility of a severe sentence is an important factor in assessing flight risk. *See United States v. Jackson,* 823 F.2d 4, 7 (2d Cir. 1987); *United States v. Cisneros,* 328 F.3d 610, 618 (10th Cir. 2003) (defendant was a flight risk because her knowledge of the seriousness of the charges against her gave her a strong incentive to abscond); *United States v. Townsend,* 897 F.2d 989, 995 (9th Cir. 1990) ("Facing the much graver penalties possible under the present indictment, the defendants have an even greater incentive to consider flight."). The defendant also does not keep assets in his name and, through his connections and followers, has access to millions of dollars and a private island.

Moreover, the risk of flight and dangerousness is further supported by every one of the Bail Reform Act factors. First, the defendant is charged with very serious crimes that involve sex trafficking of vulnerable women through coercion and manipulation, tactics the defendant has mastered over decades.

Second, the evidence against the defendant is exceedingly strong. The government has spoken to more than a dozen women who have been victimized by the defendant, as well as many other witnesses. Their statements have been corroborated, including by the defendant's own emails and electronic communications.

Third, the defendant's personal characteristics demonstrate that he is someone who is both a risk of flight and a danger to the community. As described above, he has spent decades pretending to be a renunciate while scamming people out of money and living a secret life of luxury. He has also previously directed others to falsify records to be used in a civil lawsuit and sent "cease and desist" letters to witnesses, actions which evince a willingness to obstruct justice.

With respect to the danger he poses (as relevant to both the third and fourth factors of the Bail Reform Act), the allegations in the complaint speak for themselves, and are the culmination of decades of abusing women and girls through manipulation and coercion and, at times, physical violence. The extent of his brazenness is demonstrated by the fact that he identified his adherents as "slaves" and had them branded with his initials. If released, the defendant poses a risk to numerous women, including many DOS slaves who still believe they are under his control. There is a very real concern that the defendant may attempt—either directly or indirectly through his slaves—to intimidate possible witnesses against him into silence.

CONCLUSION

For the reasons set forth above, the government intends to request that the defendant be removed in custody to the Eastern District of New York when he appears for arraignment in the Northern District of Texas tomorrow. In the event that bail proceedings take place before this Court, the government will seek a permanent order of detention. The government submits that the defendant poses a danger to the community and a risk of flight. There is no condition or combination of conditions that will assure the safety of the community, the defendant's return to court, or his compliance with the Court's directives.

Accordingly, the government requests that the defendant be permanently detained pending trial.

Respectfully submitted,

/s/ Richard P. Donoghue

RICHARD P. DONOGHUE
United States Attorney
Eastern District of New York

PSYCHOLOGICAL PROFILE
OF A MODERN CULT LEADER

White Male
Mid to late 30s
Underachiever
May have been fired from several jobs
Cannot maintain steady employment
Troubled childhood – lack of parental attention
Narcissist
Near photographic memory
Craves attention
May partake in culturally unacceptable sexual
  practices
Charming, uses a cloak of charm
Psychopathic tendencies
Excessive self-aggrandizement based on
  childhood trauma, needs to compensate for
  childhood
When caught in lie or misdeed, will attempt to
  justify the act
No qualms about soliciting monetary donations
Prefers to live on donations from others, than via
  gainful employment

LETTER FROM FORMER MEMBER OF NXIVM AND SCIENTOLOGY

From: XXXXX
To: XXXXXX

Regarding Scientology and Raniere, I was a well versed high-level Scientologist in the 1970s. I defected in '80 when Ron Hubbard was no longer running the organization.

In the early 2000s, I took two courses In Albany. First a five-day and then a 16-day. I then went to V-week. I was amazed at the level of joy, well-being, and superior ability that I witnessed and was I fascinated by the group.

I was amazed that the NXIVM program directly and overtly made great use of terminology from Scientology. There were at least 10 direct words and major concepts directly taken without even an attempt to disguise them or where they came from.

I will list only a few of them here: Suppressive, Pro-survival, Source, Gradient.

When I saw these things, I was very amazed because the explanations were very good and the same as Ron Hubbard. I was fascinated seeing these terms used. As I was fully separated from Scientology, it didn't bother me that these terms and concepts were taken from it and I felt that they were made good use of, at least at first.

So, I mentioned to Prefect (Nancy Salzman) that these were Scientology terms. She immediately told me that no, they were only from Keith and any resemblance to Scientology was purely coincidental. I assured her that this could not be possible, as the terms were defined with the exact words and concepts written by Hubbard. She was not interested in my statements. Therefore, I knew that fraud was involved and that Keith was lying to say that he developed NXIVM, with himself as the only 'source'. I saw no reason for his denial.

Here is a very interesting thing. The term "suppressive" in Scientology is exactly as Prefect defined it in her original video, as seen in the first five-day course. In fact, the detailed description of how one *becomes* a 'suppressive' was the best I have ever heard.

However, the terrible thing, is that in both cults, that term is misunderstood and misused on people as punishment and has been used to do great harm.

I tried to explain (this to Prefect) as I heard more and more terms lifted from Scientology. I never went back to the group after the delightful V-week experience, as I knew that Keith and his organization, whatever and however it started out, was a fraud and copied Scientology.

Another clue was the opera performed during V-week and it was touted as Vanguards' favorite opera. It was Sweeney Todd – about a man who grinds up people's bodies and sells them as meat pies!

ALTERNATIVE THEORY

Okay, so we reviewed the material, the background on Keith, the usual suspects, the FBI Affidavit and Investigation, and witness statements. There is one more aspect about this case.

I hesitated to place this material in the book, because it would be provocative and controversial. But, the theory needs to be presented nonetheless. Keith Raniere is a quirky dude. Walks like a monkey, has sex slaves, brands women, insists on obedience – almost worship. And the numerical structure of the Grandmaster/Slavemaster/Slaves pyramid was 666.

And if we open our Bibles for a minute...to the Revelation of St. John of Patmos in the New Testament...

"The whole world was filled with wonder and followed the beast." Revelation 13:3

- Raniere has a devoted world-wide following

"People worshiped the dragon because he had given authority to the beast, and they also worshiped the beast and asked, 'Who is like the beast? Who can wage war against it?'" Revelation 13:4

- Raniere claims supernatural abilities – strength, intelligence, speed – that have caused many to worship him as the Vanguard.

"All inhabitants of the earth will worship the beast."
Revelation 13:8

- Raniere demands worship and unflagging loyalty from all members. Raniere compares himself to Jesus Christ.

"Because of the signs it was given power to perform on behalf of the first beast, it deceived the inhabitants of the earth. It ordered them to set up an image in honor of the beast who was wounded by the sword and yet lived."
Revelation 13:14

- Raniere's followers believe he will be released from prison shortly, in essence, that he will perform a miracle and get off on all charges.

"It also forced all people, great and small, rich and poor, free and slave, to receive a mark." Revelation 13:16

- Raniere burns his mark, his initials, on his slaves.

"So that they could not buy or sell unless they had the mark, which is the name of the beast." Revelation 13:17

- NXIVM encourages members to start businesses in order to create a secret worldwide economy for NXIVM members. To transact in this economy, one must have Vanguard's mark. The mark burned onto the NXIVM slaves is 'KR' – Keith Raniere's initials.

"This calls for wisdom. Let the person who has insight calculate the number of the beast, for it is the number of a man. That number is 666." Revelation 13:18

- Raniere created his sex slave pyramid to be organized in 6s. One Grandmaster with 6 slavemasters. Each slavemaster would then have 6 slaves beneath them. Each of those slaves would then have 6 slaves each. So, the pods are organized in a numerical sequence of 666. And, the FBI reports use the term 'pod'. Instead, what if we use the word 'coven'? So, this would be a coven of female sex slaves, branded with the mark, organized into a 666.

****

What if Keith Raniere is so far gone, that he believes himself to be the anti-Christ? There are many similarities, in what Keith demanded from his followers and slaves, to the Biblical scriptures in the Revelation of St. John.

We have the branding, the mark of the Beast, the businesses, the ability to perform miracles, the meetings with heads of state, and the number of the Beast – Keith's number – 666.

Could Keith be so insane, he actually thinks he's fulfilling a Biblical prophecy? Remember that walk? The funny Keith walk?

Keith Raniere walks on the balls of his feet. He curls his toes to walk and shifts side to side. I call it a monkey walk. What if it's a Devil's walk? Isn't that how a man would move, if he didn't have feet but walked on cloven hooves? Isn't the Devil supposed to have cloven hooves? But walk around like a man – searching for sex slaves, hungry to steal their souls? At least, that is what the legends from New England say.

So, what do you think?

vincit lux tenebris

Made in the USA
San Bernardino, CA
01 March 2019